more than
Salt and Pepper

more than
Salt and Pepper

Caren McSherry

25 YEARS OF SPICING UP THE KITCHEN

foreword by Bill Good

whitecap

Dedication

To the enthusiastic, loyal students I have taught over the past 25 years. Without your thirst for culinary adventure in cooking, my journey would not have brought me this far. To all of you, here is the fruition of 25 years of passion.

Editor: Lesley Cameron
Proofreader: Marial Shea
Book design: Roberta Batchelor
Food stylist: Murray Bancroft
Food preparation: Susan Meister
Cover and food photography: Ryan Sullivan, Purdy and Co., London, England
www.purdyandcompany.com
Food photography assistant: Corina Flahr
Digital product photography: Ryan McNair and Corina Flahr
Illustration: Jacqui Thomas

PRINTED AND BOUND IN CANADA

National Library of Canada Cataloguing in Publication Data

McSherry, Caren, 1952-
  More than salt and pepper

  Includes index.
  ISBN 1-55285-399-3

  1. Cookery. I. Title.
TX714.M363 2002   641.5   C2002-910986-8

The publisher acknowledges the support of the Canada Council and the Cultural Services Branch of the Government of British Columbia in making this publication possible. We acknowledge the financial support of the Government of Canada through the Book Publishing Industry Development Program for our publishing activities.

contents

Acknowledgements

To begin with, thank you seems so inadequate an expression for such a volume of appreciation. It is with the utmost gratitude and respect that I give thanks to the many people who have given me the pleasure of working with them. As with all successful endeavors, it is the dedicated people I've worked with over the years who have helped bring this project to fruition.

My mother Clara was and still is the "Mr. Fix It" of my world. She has hammered, nailed, papered and orchestrated every cooking school move I have experienced. She has always recruited great assistants to help her execute the plans. Robert Lawrence and Patrick Hartney are two of the many who helped put our school together.

I have a spectacular team of sôus-chefs that has stood bravely over the many years, each of us gaining knowledge from one another. I thank them all. Pauline Thistlewood-Jones was one of my very first sôus-chefs. I don't know how she endured my teasing, but you rock, Pauline. Mark Wells polished his skills with me. I was lucky enough to teach the entire Osachoff family and one by one, David, Lois and Ruth all became competent members of the team—and Ruth still is! Cindy Burridge was the backbone of the school's administration and my right arm for many years. Doreen Corday, my good friend, overwhelming organizer and tremendous cook, still holds top rank at the school. If you need it done, call Doreen! Jack Stoughton's passion for spicy food had his cleaver on the chopping board for a few years. Susan Meister, who currently directs the school, has been a tremendous asset, keeping the classes full of excitement, style and learning. To Christine Blackwood, owner of Alternative Uniforms, for the chef's coat that appears in the front cover photograph. To Kosta at The Salmon Shop, for his generosity in supplying the fresh fish for the photo shoot.

The thanks can go on forever with people and friends who have been a part of my life and believe in what I do. Lana Quinn, Michelle Boudreau and Jenny Ambrose, thank you. One of the key people who always, always has a smile on her face for everyone, Amarilde Lourença. Obrigado Fofa. These friends have all been part of the 25 years, both past and present.

The School is strengthened by The Gourmet Warehouse, which has what I think is the best team in the city. Headed by Steve McKinley, an excellent chef and hugely knowledgeable about food products and their applications. The entire crew works together: thanks go to Gerald Coutts, Joyce Ross, Giselle Arcand, James Johnstone, Sheri Hackwell and Anne Rose. Imee Borja, who tries to expel me each day at 3 PM, is indeed a saint. She also holds the purse strings and is an enormous support to me.

Ryan McNair, who tirelessly chases excellence in the name of our website, has been wonderful in not only being a great guy but in making us look good. Robert McCullough, my dear friend, who happens to be the publisher, is first and foremost a foodie at heart. I have nicknamed him the condiment king because he owns every quality condiment on this continent and others, I'm sure. When I asked him if a 25th anniversary book would work and more importantly sell, he was very supportive. Thank you for your belief.

Sophie Hunter, who saved me from drowning in a sea of editing, and Roberta Batchelor whose creativity is amazing, Robin Rivers who I drove crazy by constantly going out of town, sorry! Thanks to Michael Burch, head honcho at Whitecap, for putting up with my cheekiness and actually printing the book.

Ruy Paes-Braga, Vice President of the Four Season's Hotel, for allowing me to realize my two book launches in the ultimate of properties. Style is everything. You are the best, thank you. Karen Barnaby for her expertise.

Corina Flahr for assisting in photography and cooking during the marathon week of food photography. Murray Bancroft for making the food stylish and teaching us break-dancing during lunch hour.

Susi Owen for waving her magic wand and making the photographer a reality. Her agency (Purdy and Co.) made Ryan Sullivan possible. Ryan's brilliance, calmness and great personality made everyone at ease as he clicked the shutter hundreds of times.

There is always someone left out and never with intent, so I am apologizing now. Sorry if I missed you.

My two best friends, Diane Lawrence and Susan Meister, have listened to me whine and poured wine during this endless journey of recipe recollection. What would I do without you? xoxoxo

In closing, a giant thanks to my family, my husband José Valagao and the entire purpose of my life, Christina and Jason, you are the greatest kids a mom could have—even with the fighting! I love you more than Disneyland!

Foreword

Welcome to Caren's world.

I first met Caren when she was a guest on my radio program. I was immediately smitten with her energy and enthusiasm and I became a big fan when I enjoyed some of her many excellent recipes. Caren believes in the KISS formula: Keep It Simple Stupid. Seriously, if you can read, you can follow a McSherry recipe and become a great cook. We did several items together and Caren became a regular on my CKNW radio show. I look forward to her visits every Thursday. We've become good friends and have enjoyed many meals at her house with José and the kids, at our house, and in several Lower Mainland restaurants that Caren loves to promote.

She promotes good food and she loves to encourage people to sample local markets and learn about local producers of food products. Caren McSherry lives to the fullest. She shares her love of life with her love of food, and yes, fine wine, too, which she enjoys with her husband and partner José.

When Caren isn't on the radio, or on television, she's teaching people how to cook in her much-in-demand cooking school, or selling a new pot, or the world's best oven mitt at the Gourmet Warehouse.

This human hurricane will blow into any room or studio and clear it of any sign of stuffiness in about ten seconds. She finds time to be mother, partner, business woman, friend and daughter and she does it all with flair. She is generous to a fault with her time, and is constantly in demand to help raise money for many charities. When she's not cooking or teaching someone how to cook, she's skiing in Whistler or holidaying in the sun.

Learning to cook with Caren isn't just about finding a recipe for a meal. It's a recipe for life. Life with fun, life with flair. Caren believes in having a good time and making the most of time with family and friends, and she can show you how to make the most of your kitchen. Enjoy! Salute!

I can't think of anybody I know who gets more out of life and gives back more than Caren McSherry. How she managed to find the time to put out another book boggles my mind, but she's done it and I know that if you take the time to make even one of the recipes in this latest chapter in the life and times of Caren McSherry, you will be a proud host.

Bill Good

Introduction

November 1978 marked the birth of my cooking school. Humble but stylish, it was on East Georgia Street in Vancouver. Fresh faced and full of confidence, I emerged from Cordon Bleu, which had just released the latest crop of eager culinary graduates onto the hungry public. I stood bravely in front of six wide-eyed students, full of anxiety and ready to share what I thought was cutting edge. I remember preparing classic mayonnaise (God knows why, as Hellmann's had it perfected). It didn't break and I successfully, but certainly not confidently, got through my first payment-based cooking class.

Twenty-five years and 26,000 well-fed students later, the trepidation and nervousness have long gone, but my energy, love and, most of all, passion for what I do have not. *More than Salt and Pepper* is not simply a collection of creative recipes worked over and over in cooking classes, but an understanding of how food has moved forward by becoming sophisticated yet simple and comforting, all at the same time.

Fast forward 25 years: food and teaching now embrace a new focus. Purchased quality condiments, elevated salts and indigenous peppers are allowed, even accepted and applauded when they are good. Gone are the days of night school classes where crowded pick forks submerged cubes of meat into a pot of lukewarm fat. Emerging on the food scene is a host of vibrant, energetic teachers bursting with information, ideas and an abundance of nutritional savvy. Many of them jump from the pages of this book, and I thank them all for being involved.

My school has brought me immense pleasure. Through its longevity and reputation, I have had many opportunities: forming fabulous friendships, sailing with Crystal Cruise Lines as their host teacher, preparing the launch dinner at Flora Springs Winery for the opening of the Napa Valley Wine Auction, and leading amazing food and wine tours throughout Europe.

Hosting the first food and wine radio broadcast with CKNW/98 was an exciting challenge. Although it lasted a short 20 months, it was a fantastic experience and I thank Ian Koeningsfest for the opportunity. When one door closes, another often opens and it led to me becoming a weekly guest on the Bill Good show on CKNW. Thursdays at 1 PM have become the highlight of my week, not just to talk food but to share with a great broadcaster and journalist. Our weekly chat is printed as a featured recipe in *TV WEEK MAGAZINE*. Better yet, Bill and his wife Georgy have become great friends with me and my family, sharing dinners, wine, conversation and cooking.

My good fortune to be involved with Robert McCullough and *The Girls Who Dish* series has also furthered the pleasure of my career.

Being a native Vancouverite, I have experienced a good career in a great city. I don't regret anything, other than not having long skinny legs or being a ramp model in Paris.

Food has a way of bringing people together in spite of religion, political beliefs or social status. It is a greater leveler, for regardless of who or what we are, we can break bread together and be thankful for the occasion—and more importantly, the memory.

truths about

Balsamic Vinegar

Born centuries ago in Modena and the Reggio Emilia areas of Italy, "balsam" was reserved for emperors, noblemen and kings. Steeped in ancient traditions and extremely valuable, this thick aromatic nectar of the gods was jealously guarded by the small number of families that produced it. Consumption was limited to special occasions. It was customary, for example, to honor a daughter entering marriage with a small cask of vinegar as part of her dowry.

Today, there are few people who have not heard of or tasted balsamic vinegar. However, it still remains the most misunderstood of all the vinegars.

TRADIZIONALE

Traditional Balsamic Vinegar of Modena is made from the fermentation of must from white Trebbiano grapes. The must is cooked on direct flames in open vats until it is reduced by half. It is then placed in casks of wood where it acetifies through natural fermentation. The casks are placed in lofts where the vinegar intensifies through evaporation and is decanted in a series of different woods: oak, chestnut, cherry ash and finally mulberry. Beginning with 12 years and moving up past 25 years, the length of time that the vinegar is aged in the wood determines the quality and the price. After it is aged, the vinegar is bottled in spherical glass bottles with a thick rectangular base. Each bottle holds 100 mL.

All producers must submit their "Tradizionale" to a consortium, which judges the vinegar on the merits set forth by a panel. Once the vinegar passes, it is awarded the special "Tradizionale" bottle, in which it is bottled, numbered and identified by producer. The designation of the traditional bottle reflects the laborious, coveted and time-honored position that the vinegar deserves.

It is important to understand that "Tradizionale" is very different from Balsamic Vinegar of Modena. To be true aceto balsamico, it must be produced and bottled in Modena. Since "Tradizionale" is very expensive, Balsamic Vinegar of Modena has become the affordable ambassador for the Italian vinegar.

BALSAMIC VINEGAR OF MODENA

In order to produce enough to meet world demand, the consortium has allowed significant differences. The must is only partially fermented and the addition of previously aged 10-year-old vinegar is allowed along with a small amount of caramel. The aging period is the largest difference, although it must still be done in wood. The total aging of Balsamic Vinegar of Modena can vary from 6 months up to several years. The decanting is not specific; unlike Tradizionale, producers are free to choose any bottle. Only a handful of producers are qualified to use the name Balsamic Vinegar of Modena and the consortium of Italy has awarded their integrity with special labels that signify their status.

Despite these standards, confusion continues, which is why the Balsamic Italian Tasters' Association has designed a classification system to develop consumer confidence in a market where uncertainly prevails. There are four levels, signified by a varying number of vine leaves.

One leaf identifies the vinegar as inexpensive and recommended for everyday use.

Two leaves indicates a smoother, more complex flavor, suited for barbecue or garden vegetables.

Three leaves indicates a far more intense, sweet vinegar, great to finish sauces or soup or to drizzle on cheese.

Four leaves is exceptionally dense, almost syrupy vinegar that can be sipped as a digestive as is done in Italy.

This rating system is very new and will take time to implement. If you are ever in doubt about what to purchase, I highly recommend the Aceto Balsamico di Modena Del Duca from the estate of the Groseli Family, one of the finest balsamics in Italy.

Butter

Butter is generally purchased three ways—salted, unsalted and European style.

SALTED BUTTER

Salted Butter is the most commonly available. The salt is usually added for North American taste preference and preservation. The salt masks any taste of rancidity. In North America, we are quite careless about butter, which is interesting because of how diligent we are with other dairy products like milk, cream, eggs and cheese. We would never leave milk or cream out overnight but butter is overlooked.

For example, we tend to leave butter out in small dishes. I believe this is to ensure that it is always spreadable. We tend to forget it is perishable and requires refrigeration. The salt can mask flavor changes brought on by irregular refrigeration.

Salted butter is less expensive than unsalted because the salt allows more water to be "held" in the butter.

UNSALTED BUTTER

No salt is added to unsalted butter, so the flavor is one that requires a little taste adaptation. Unsalted butter is always the butter of choice in cooking and especially baking. The lack of salt always allows the home cook or chef to determine the salt content. It is quite often sold frozen.

EUROPEAN STYLE

This is a delicious version of unsalted butter. Active cultures—similar to yogurt or sour cream—are added to the cream before churning, giving the butter an almost sweet flavor. It is by far the tastiest and costliest of the three types of butter. It is wonderful on fresh-baked bread and scones. The flavor ripens over time, just like a good cheese.

Chipotle Chilies

Chilies are rapidly becoming a major player as a flavor component in our new North American cooking. Of the hundreds of chilies available, the current 15 minutes of fame seems to be shining on the chipotle.

It is actually the common ripened jalapeño. What makes it special is that the jalapeños are smoked over a wood fire, which completely alters their taste dimension. The depth of taste gives off hints of chocolate and spice.

The most common way to purchase them is canned. They come packed in an adobo sauce which can also be used in recipes.

Chocolate

The cocoa bean is the fruit of a tropical tree, *Theobroma cacao*. The quality of chocolate will depend on the origin and quality of the beans. The best chocolate is made from the purest and best cocoa that can be found. Beans come from many countries including Trinidad, Ghana, Madagascar, Venezuela and Papua New Guinea.

The cocoa beans are roasted and shelled, leaving the centers, called nibs. They are pulverized or ground into a smooth liquid that's called chocolate liquor. When cooled, it forms solid blocks.

Pure chocolate liquor is dark and bitter, with only two components—cocoa solids and cocoa butter. The solids give chocolate its flavor, and the cocoa butter its smooth mouth feel. Chocolate liquor contains a little more than half (50% to 58%) cocoa butter, the rest being solids. By increasing the cocoa butter, chocolate with a better sheen and smoother texture results. A high-pressure filter process breaks down chocolate liquor and separates the solids from the butter. The chocolate can then be manipulated to produce a range of styles.

UNSWEETENED

This is the very familiar baking and cooking chocolate that can be purchased easily in supermarkets everywhere. It should not be confused with bittersweet chocolate, as it has absolutely no sugar and is much too strong for an eating chocolate. It is commonly used for making brownies, fudge and sauces. It is the closest we can get to buying pure chocolate liquor since it contains nothing more than cocoa solids and cocoa butter.

BITTERSWEET

Lucky you if you can find it at 99%! This chocolate has a strong flavor and does contain chocolate liquor, cocoa butter, sugar and vanilla. It has a more pronounced chocolate flavor and far less sweetness. Scharffen Berger and most European varieties are good choices.

SEMI-SWEET

At 62-70% cocoa butter, it is very comparable to bittersweet and they can be easily interchanged. The significant difference is that bittersweet is more pronounced and stronger in chocolate flavor simply because of the 99% content of chocolate liquor and, of course, less sugar. You need not alter any recipe when interchanging either semi- or bittersweet chocolate. Scharffen Berger, Lindt, Ghirardelli, Valrhona and Callebaut are all quality choices.

MILK

Milk chocolate actually contains dry milk, as well as sugar, chocolate liquor and cocoa butter. The addition of these ingredients makes it far milder and the preferred eating chocolate, especially for children. The higher content of cocoa liquor in the darker chocolates lends a more complex and intense flavor which milk chocolate does not possess. It does, however, shine in cookies and mousses or whenever a low heat is present. It does not like high heat, as it has a tendency to thicken and lump when melted too quickly and the milk tends to burn easily.

WHITE

Legally, white chocolate cannot be termed such because it does not contain chocolate liquor. Most of the white chocolate that we know has none. When you purchase white chocolate, ensure that the key ingredient aside from the sugar, vanilla, etc, is cocoa butter. Without this addition, it will be labeled "coating," which contains palm kernel, cottonseed or soybean oil. Note that in melting white chocolate, a double boiler is imperative because if the heat is too high the chocolate will simply coagulate into a big lumpy mass. It is best used in mousses and sauces.

COCOA POWDER

There are two types of cocoa powder, natural unsweetened or Dutch alkalized. The Dutch version was founded by a man named van Houten, who developed a technique to remove most of the cocoa butter from the nibs. The process, called "Dutching," lowered the pH and gave a darker color and richer taste to the cocoa powder. This makes it a huge favorite with chocolatiers and pastry makers alike, because of the deep dark colour and flavor. Because Dutched cocoa is neutral, it does not react with baking soda. It must be used in recipes calling for baking power, unless other acidic ingredients in sufficient quantities are present, such as buttermilk or sour cream. Droste, Lindt, Valrhona and Bensdorf are all examples of Dutch Processed Cocoa.

Harissa

Harissa is a fiery hot condiment used to spice up foods. Primarily consumed in Tunisia and Morocco, this chili-based paste can be purchased in jars, tubes or small tins. Once opened, refrigerate it and maintain it with a thin covering of olive oil on top. It is great as a rub on meats or shellfish, stirred into a soup or stew for an extra kick or simply served as a condiment alongside your favorite foods. I love it with pizza!

Lemon Grass

Originating in Southeast Asia, this fragrant reed provides a lemon scent in many dishes. Thai curries, soups, salads, even desserts find that unique flavor note that only lemon grass can deliver. Use only the inner white part for your dishes, as the outer layer is fibrous and thick in texture.

The whole reed can be trimmed, cut into long strips and used as a flavorful skewer when you want a hint of lemon accenting your dish. Widely available in Asian markets, quality produce stores and Chinatown.

Lentilles du Puy

Originating more than 10,000 years ago, lentils are rich with protein, vitamin B and iron.

Depending on the species, the color of lentils can range from jet black to a glossy orange. Sixty percent of the world's supply comes from India and Turkey, but the darling of the crowd, lentilles du Puy, is the hardest to come by. In the French region of Haute Loire, a tiny town named Le Puy produces a tiny firm grey-green legume which chefs love because of its texture and its ability to hold its shape when cooked. Fabulous in soups, salads or beds for crowning main courses, du Puy lentils triple in volume when cooked.

They have been granted an Appellation d'Origine Contrôlée from the French government, designating Le Puy as the only region producing these lentils.

Lentilles du Puy

Olive Oil

Olive oil is priced and graded by a global hierarchy whose income is in excess of $5 billion a year. With the Mediterranean basin providing the largest production in the world, it is Spain that ranks as the world's leader, accounting for 45% of the total. Italy is next with 25%. However, they must import, as domestic production cannot meet home consumption demands. Greece, Turkey, Tunisia and Portugal follow in declining order. Although in North America we hail California as a contributor, it actually accounts for a mere .5% of the world's total.

The European Community grades all of its oil through an acidity evaluation—a chemical test—followed by human tastings by highly trained officials.

EXTRA VIRGIN

There are certain criteria an oil must meet in order to qualify under the title "extra virgin." The olives must undergo only cold pressing, possess an acidity level of less than 1% and have a perfectly balanced taste. The IOOC (International Olive Oil Council) has set the taste standard by which these oils are judged.

The olives are picked, sorted and washed, then crushed and pressed with a traditional stone mill. It is imperative that no heat or chemicals are added to this crushing to extend or alter the oil. The acidity is then measured by a simple chemical reaction. It must also display a rich fruitiness.

UNFILTERED OLIVE OIL

This oil is certainly not new to Europe, but is a unique purchase here in North America. The best oil in Europe is most often the one that is not sold, but coveted for family, friends and special guests.

It is usually believed that olive oil must be deep green to be a quality purchase. It is not necessarily so in olive oil producing areas. This special oil comes with a cloudy appearance, almost as if something is wrong. Nothing could be farther from the truth as it is generally the first run of oil, even before the olives see their first press. If you are fortunate enough to be in the area during this gathering, buy as much as you can carry—liquid gold in aroma and flavor. Travel and demand have brought the unfiltered version to this continent. Be aware when you purchase it, it will be cloudy, it will have a sediment and a murkiness lingering around the bottom of the bottle. Quite simply put, it is unfiltered. The flavor is amazing. Consume it, don't save it.

VIRGIN OR PURE OLIVE OIL

This is the most widely marketed grade of oil, primarily because it generally costs less than extra virgin. It can combine extra virgin and virgin but must comply with an acidity test of less than 1.5%.

POMACE

The absolute lowest grade of oil, it is a blend of pure and refined pomace. Pomace is a chemical solvent that is used to extract any residual oil left in olive paste after its final extraction. It does not possess any of the fruitiness that is usually associated with olive oil. It is its minimal cost that attracts consumers. However, it should be noted that this is not olive oil and only in North America can it be labeled "Pomace Olive Oil." It is the author's opinion that pomace is not an enhancement to anything that you cook. I would avoid it.

Peppers

FIVE BLENDED PEPPERCORNS

Five blended peppercorns is a unique blend of four peppercorns, including black, green, white and pink. The fifth pepper is not pepper at all, but whole allspice, which acts as the aromatic softener, reducing the pepperiness of the four corns. This blend provides a flavorful, complex addition to most dishes where pepper is integral in the recipe, but the bold upfront pepper taste is not required. It is wonderful on just about everything from soups to salads.

GRAINS OF PARADISE

Cultivated in Africa and once thought to be the first cousins of the pepper that we know today. They look like small seeds and produce a mild peppery flavor. They are not commonly available.

GREEN PEPPERCORNS

Picked before white or black pepper as it is the first color that the berry shows. Most commonly they are purchased brined or freeze-dried. Fresh green peppercorns are not available in North America, with the exception of some exclusive Asian import stores that air freight them. Thailand is abundant with fresh green peppercorns as they are a staple in green curry sauce.

ITALIAN CRACKED PEPPER

An unusual location descriptor for this coarse cracked pepper, as Italy is not known as a producer of pepper. It is, however, a big player in world cuisine. The grade and size of the pepper enhances the food of this country, which is gutsy, rustic and full of big, honest flavors. This pepper is cracked coarse to reflect the style of Italian cooking. Sprinkle liberally on foods that can absorb the heady boldness of this cooking pepper.

LAMPONG PEPPER

Lampong peppercorns are grown in Indonesia. The vines produce small-fruited peppercorns that take on a greyish color during storage. The pepper is harvested green by plucking the whole pepper spike in the moment when the very first berry starts to turn red and storing the berries overnight at room temperature. They are left to ferment—a process similar to the fermentation of tea leaves—and then spread out to dry. Lampong pepper is hot.

MALABAR PEPPER

Malabar black peppercorns from India have for many years ranked as the best grade of pepper available. They pale in color and aroma to their big brother the Tellicherry, but do not discount the power they pack. For many successive years, Malabar peppercorns were the number one choice for chefs and home cooks everywhere. They're great on meats, stews, root vegetables and anywhere that a strong taste of pepper is needed.

MUNTOK PEPPERCORNS

Muntok white pepper is from Malaysian-grown ripe peppercorns that are soaked in water until the pericarp loosens. The softened coating is removed by washing and rubbing, then left to dry in the sun. Long favored by the British and Dutch as the white pepper of choice, it's also used by chefs to season light-colored foods where the flavor is wanted but the color is not.

PINK PEPPERCORNS

Pink peppercorns are not really part of the pepper family at all. Its source is the Baies Rose plant. Pungent and slightly sweet, it is commonly sold brined and freeze dried. It is good in sauces and joins the group in being a member of the five pepper blend.

SARAWAK

Sarawak peppercorns are grown on the northeast coast of the Island of Borneo. Up to 80% of the crop is turned into white pepper. Black Sarawak pepper is prepared by drying the mature but still green berries in the sun for 3–4 days. After thorough drying, the berries change color to a deep mahogany brown or black. For Sarawak white pepper, fully ripened pepper berries are harvested. The berries are placed in jute bags and soaked in fresh running water for about two weeks. Then they are washed several times in rattan baskets to remove the stalks and the pericarp before sun-drying for 2–3 days. The process yields a whiter color and an extra-clean product.

SMOKED SPANISH PAPRIKA

This pepper is the fruit of the capsicum plant, originally from Central America. It was brought to Spain by Columbus. In Spain there are two main areas of production, Extremadura and Murcia. The Extremadura region, La Vera, produces a high-quality smoked paprika. This is because, before grinding, the peppers are dried using the traditional method of oak smoking. This gives them an unmistakable smoky taste.

There are three varieties of paprika: sweet, bittersweet and hot. It is also known as Pimenton de La Vera. It has been awarded a Denominación de Origen from the Spanish government. It should not be confused with Hungarian paprika as it has no close relationship or taste. The incredible natural smokiness of the paprika lends itself to dishes such as chowders, stews, eggs, poultry and soups. My favorite brand is La Chinata.

SZECHWAN

From the Sichuan province in China, it is not really a peppercorn but a pink-brown seed that grows on the prickly ash tree. It is often accompanied by small black seeds with a slightly bitter, pungent taste and an aroma like camphor. Make sure you pick out the twigs, small thorns and any visible leaves when using. A fabulous addition to Asian cooking, marinades and rubs, providing a peppery taste. If used in abundance, it can cause a numbing sensation on your tongue.

TELLICHERRY

Tellicherry is the crown prince of peppercorns. It is without a doubt the finest pepper available. An Indian corn, its size outweighs all others in its class. It is a mature grade of pepper and consequently delivers a bigger, bolder taste and incredible aroma. Tellicherry is a perfect finish to most dishes, accenting meats, salads and intense, bold sauces.

Preserved Lemon

This staple of the Moroccan kitchen is essential to many dishes. In North America, we are just beginning to romance its flavor. The lemons are pickled in salt, bay leaf and lemon juice for a minimum of three weeks. This procedure, although lengthy, renders the fruit soft. It is primarily the peel that is used for the unusual flavor it gives to stew, tagines or vinaigrettes. What a wonderful addition to your pantry.

Preserved Lemons

Risotto

Risotto is the classic rice dish of Northern Italy. "Risotto" is the name of the dish and "Arborio" is the strain of rice used to create it. The quality of Arboro rice is measured and classified by the size of the individual grains. There are very small grains that are not usually made available for export, such as comune, semi fino and fino. Super fino is the largest grain and the one most easily available in North America. In my opinion, one should never step below a super fino in the preparation of a risotto. Alternate choices of superb rice include Canaroli and the ultimate Vialone Nano. Price is definitely an indicator in these premium grades; however, the creaminess that is released from the top strains is well worth the extra cash.

Saffron

Saffron is most commonly associated with championing the flavor component in classic dishes such as Paella, Bouillabaisse and Risotto Milanese. Not restricted to savory items, saffron spreads its flavor wings to excite many classic European breads and baked items.

The best saffron originates in La Mancha, Spain, and has a reputation and dollar confirmation of being the most expensive spice in the world. Iran, India and Israel are also large producers of this valuable spice. My preference is the saffron from La Mancha, which boasts the most famed stigmas. Luis Ayala Miralles is my favorite.

Saffron is taken from the purple crocus plant, not the one we associate with the first burst of spring, but the crocus sativus. Each flower yields only three stigmas. It takes anywhere from 13,000 to 14,000 stigmas to yield a mere ounce of saffron. Only purchase the thread or whole stigmas, never, never the powder. The powdered version is very often cut with or dominated by turmeric, which will yield a bounty of color but will fail to deliver on taste. To use the threads, pound a teaspoon of them in a mortar with $^1/_2$ tsp (2.5 mL) of salt. Once you have a powder, dissolve it in a $^1/_2$ cup (120 mL) of any liquid called for in the recipe. The liquid will be bright orange and very fragrant. Store the saffron in a cool area away from direct light.

Salts

BLACK SALT

It is primarily used in Indian cooking. Sold in rock form and ground in a mortar, its color is almost purple-black with a sulfurous odor. It is not a personal favorite.

FLEUR DE SEL

Fleur de sel is a very special gift from Mother Nature. It is created when the wind blows on the surface of the sea and the sun is warm enough to crystallize the "flowers."

Once the sun has dried the salt and the crystal forms, a Saunier, as he is called in France, rakes together the delicate flakey crystals that form on the water's surface. This is known to us as fleur de sel, "flower of salt." It is always dampish in feel and slightly grey in color.

HAWAIIAN AND RED SALT

A red-orange salt crystal that obtains its color from the natural red lava of Kauai and Molokai. I find the flavor rather earthy due to the lava.

KOSHER SALT

Kosher salt has half the saltiness of sea salt and is often the salt of choice in professional kitchens. The grain is uniform and the taste marries well in marinades. A mined salt, free of chemicals and additives, it is an excellent choice for pickling and general cooking.

MALDON SALT

Maldon salt, from the coast of England, is a quality sea salt that resembles large flakes rather than crystals. Quite briney in taste but fabulous over salads and sliced garden vegetables. It has a very pronounced salty flavor.

SEL GRIS

"Grey salt" is a large, hard and moist crystallized sea salt that hails from Brittany. It is very dirty grey in color and moist to the touch, and it makes a wonderful addition to big game meats, duck and coarse veggies like Swiss chard and cabbage.

Truffles

Truffles are a fungus that grows primarily at the base of oak, hazelnut, willow and poplar trees. Long considered a gourmand's delight, an aphrodisiac and claimed by many a truffle connoisseur to be as good as sex. They impregnate the atmosphere with an aroma you will never forget. They are best consumed fresh—sliced paper thin and served over pasta, mild meats or vegetables. France, Italy and Spain boast the world's choicest truffles, with Yugoslavia, China, Turkey, North Africa and the United States following behind with a lesser quality. Truffles have many varieties, with summer truffle being one of the more affordable. Its flavor is pleasant, although not nearly as heady and sexy as the white truffles from Alba.

BLACK TRUFFLES

Black truffles are chestnut black and resemble a lump of coal. They are generally about the size of a golf ball, but can grow as large as baseballs. They are fresh from November to March and best eaten in slightly warm dishes.

OREGONIAN

Small in size and really not a true truffle at all, the Oregonian is very affordable for the folks from the Pacific Northwest. However, they do not possess that unforgettable aroma of their royal cousins as their fragrance is more along the lines of earth and mushrooms.

WHITE TRUFFLES

White truffles are Italian in descent and creamy beige in color. They are the costliest of all species, commanding upward of $3,000 per pound. They fill the room with a heady, unforgettable aroma. White truffles are best eaten fresh and sliced paper thin.

TRUFFLE HONEY

Truffle honey is a classic condiment originating in the Tuscan area of Italy, but now produced in many other areas. Golden honey is blended with white truffle oil to create an intense, sweet, intoxicating blend. It is a marriage of flavor that can only be understood by the senses. You must try it with cheese, prosciutto, crusty bread, and don't forget the red wine! You won't regret it and will remember the heady flavor sensation forever!

TRUFFLE OIL

Truffle oil is olive, safflower or grapeseed oil uniquely blended with truffle. The fundamental difference is whether it is "infused" or "flavored." Flavored is just that—a quick scent and a light taste that does not last long. Infused is more costly and consequently delivers a huge truffle scent and flavor. A quality brand I use is La Madia Regale. It is so worth the expense. Expect to pay anywhere from $9 to $20 for 100 mL. It must be refrigerated after opening and will keep up to a year. Use it drizzled on risotto, mashed potatoes or sprinkled on anything mushroom.

Vanilla

Vanilla is, without a doubt, the most popular flavor in the world. The vanilla bean or pod originated in Mexico and was used by the Totonaco Indians until the Aztecs conquered them. As history goes, it was originally used with cocoa beans to make a delicious drink called "chocolatl." When the drink made its way to Europe, it was a luxury that only the noble and rich could afford.

It wasn't until 1793 that the original vine found its way out of Mexico to be planted on the Island of Reunion. In this region of the world, the beans are referred to as Bourbon. The most important growing regions are the Bourbon Islands, Indonesia, Mexico, Tongo and Tahiti.

Vanilla pods are the fruit of an orchid plant. Although there are thousands of varieties of orchid, the vanilla plant is the only one with edible fruit. Pollination is done by hand and it takes 3–4 years for the vine to produce fruit. The flavor and aroma of vanilla varies from region to region and is influenced by how the beans are produced.

INDONESIA

Indonesian vanilla is generally considered to be of lower quality than that of other producing areas. Although Indonesia is the second largest producer of vanilla, the harvesting and curing practices are not as honored as those of other areas. Used commercially and for lower-priced vanillas that are marked "pure."

MADAGASCAR BOURBON

Madagascar is the largest producer of beans and they are the most affordable variety. They have a rich sweet flavor and can be used whenever pure vanilla is called for in a recipe.

MEXICAN

Mexican vanilla, contrary to popular belief, is quite scarce. There has been a sharp decline in production as the areas in which the beans grow have given way to oil and orange grove production, both of which are far more profitable than the high-maintenance vanilla bean.

It has a mild smooth flavor and marries perfectly with cinnamon. It is great for cookies, cakes and sauces. Real Mexican vanilla is much more costly than Madagascan and Indonesian vanilla.

TAHITIAN

Tahitian is the most expensive variety of all the vanillas. It possesses an exotic fruity, floral flavor and aroma. It is wonderful with fruit-based items, but does not hold as well for baked goods. It is a great choice for ice cream.

PASTE

Very new to the vanilla market, the paste can also be used one-for-one to its liquid counterpart. Because of the fine seeds incorporated in the paste, it is a perfect application for crème brûlée, custards, crème anglaise, soufflés and any light-colored desserts where the real presence of vanilla seeds is required. It is my personal favorite.

POWDERED

A white powder formulated without sugar or alcohol is used on a one-for-one exchange with the liquid variety. Commonly used as a beverage topping, for adding to pancakes, cocoa, muffin and bread mixes and where your dish may be color sensitive to the liquid extract. It is perfect for frostings and meringues.

appetizers

José's Herbed Olives

Olives were once popular only in Spanish tapas bars, bistros in Provence and on Portuguese dinner tables. I've mentioned previously that once we North Americans taste a good thing, there is no letting go. My husband José is a Portuguese national. His life before Canada was, and still is, olives, fish, salt cod and wine. I've managed to embrace it all with gusto, except for salt cod. These olives are truly one of his trademarks and definitely worth making.

In a large bowl, mix together the garlic, lemon slices, chili flakes, cracked pepper, rosemary, oregano and thyme. Add all the olives, stirring well to combine the flavors. Pack the olives into glass jars, cover with oil and refrigerate until ready to use. They can be served right away or will keep for several months refrigerated.

2–3	garlic cloves, chopped	2–3
1/2	lemon, cut into slices	1/2
1 tbsp	hot chili flakes	15 mL
1 tbsp	coarsely cracked pepper	15 mL
2–3	sprigs fresh rosemary, rubbed	2–3
2–3	sprigs fresh oregano, rubbed	2–3
2–3	sprigs fresh thyme, rubbed	2–3
1 cup	niçoise olives, *ARNAUD*	240 mL
1 cup	kalamata olives	240 mL
1 cup	sun-dried, oil-cured olives	240 mL
1 cup	large green olives, with pits *BELLA DI CERIGNOLA*	240 mL
1 cup	extra virgin olive oil	240 mL

MAKES 4 CUPS (960 ML)

CAREN'S ADVICE

To obtain maximum flavor and fragrance from fresh herbs, rub them between your hands to release their essential oils.

Arnaud Olives from France, and Bella di Cerignola from Italy provide an international flair to this dish.

Wendy's Spicy Nuts

Without a doubt, the tastiest, most flavorful, robust, gotta-eat-more nuts that will ever pass your lips! My friend Wendy Yackimec has, over the years, perfected a mixture of nuts and spice. She has coddled, roasted and somewhat coaxed this mixture of assorted nuts into being the perfect cocktail snack. Thanks, Wendy!

1^1/$_2$ lb	mixed unsalted nuts, such as cashews, almonds, brazil nuts, pecans, hazelnuts, pistachios and peanuts	680 g
6 tbsp	quality soy sauce	90 mL
2^1/$_2$ tbsp	grapeseed or peanut oil	37.5 mL
4^1/$_2$ tbsp	chili oil	67.5 mL
1^1/$_2$ tsp	fleur de sel or coarse sea salt (see p. 25)	7.5 mL

SERVES 6–8

Preheat oven to 350°F (175°C). Place the nuts in a large bowl and set aside. In a small bowl, mix together the soy sauce, oil, chili oil and salt. Pour this mixture over the nuts and mix well to coat evenly with seasoning.

Transfer to a large roasting pan and bake in the preheated oven for about 20 minutes or until the nuts are crispy. It is important to stir the nuts every 5–6 minutes to ensure even roasting.

Aunty Betty's Hummus

Betty Revoy, the queen of Greek and Middle Eastern cooking has graced our cooking school on several occasions. She makes, without a doubt, the best hummus this side of the Nile! Because it's quick and easy, this is an absolute perfect recipe for anyone with a hectic lifestyle and an appreciation for great-tasting food! Thanks, Betty.

1 (19 oz)	can of chickpeas, drained, and reserve liquid	1 (540 mL)
2	garlic cloves	2
3 tbsp	tahini (sesame paste)	45 mL
1	lemon, juice of	1
2 tsp	ground cumin	10 mL
1 tsp	nile spice (optional)	5 mL
to taste	freshly ground black pepper	
^{1}/$_3$ cup	extra virgin olive oil	80 mL
to taste	sea salt	
GARNISH		
^{1}/$_4$ cup	fresh parsley, finely chopped	60 mL

MAKES 2 CUPS (480 ML)

Place the drained chickpeas and the garlic in a Cuisinart and purée until smooth. If the mixture is very thick, add a little of the reserved chickpea liquid. Add the tahini, lemon juice and spices, pulse the machine until well blended. With the machine still running, slowly pour in the olive oil. The mixture should be thick like mayonnaise. Add the salt according to taste and transfer the mixture to a small serving dish. Garnish with chopped parsley. Serve with Pita Crisps (see p. 129).

Warm Chèvre Dip

Try this unique warm dip when an appetizer is required and you have no time. It is good served with French bread, crackers, sliced pears or apples. In the remote chance that there is some left over, try it as a sauce on cooked hot pasta.

³/₄ cup	sun-dried tomatoes	180 mL
¹/₃ cup	olive oil	80 mL
1	medium onion, sliced	1
1 tbsp	granulated sugar	15 mL
¹/₂–1 cup	dry white wine	120 mL–240 mL
8 oz	soft goat cheese, *WOOLWICH DAIRY*	227 mL
4 oz	firm cream cheese	115 mL
1 (14 oz)	jar artichoke hearts, drained and cut into eighths	1 (398 mL)
1	head garlic, roasted (see p. 174)	1
²/₃ cup	niçoise olives	160 mL
1 tbsp	coarsely cracked black pepper	15 mL
1	loaf of crusty French bread	1

SERVES 8–10

Dice the tomatoes and soak in enough hot water to cover for about 15 minutes or until softened. Drain and set aside. Heat the oil in a sauté pan. When the oil is hot, add the onion and cook for about 3 minutes until it begins to brown. Add the sugar and continue to cook for about 10 minutes or until the onion is dark brown and nicely caramelized. Pour in the wine and deglaze the pan, scraping all the brown flavor bits from the bottom.

Add the goat cheese, cream cheese, tomatoes, artichokes, roasted garlic, olives and pepper. Stir until the cheeses melt and the entire mixture is creamy and smooth. If it is too thick, simply adjust the consistency with the addition of more wine. Taste and adjust seasonings.

Transfer to a serving bowl and offer slices of crusty French bread.

Kerry Sear chef/owner of Cascadia, Seattle WA

Stuffed Baguette

My introduction into the real food world was in the early 1970s. I joined a Canadian charter airline called Wardair. It was there, in flight attendant training, that I met my first culinary mentor, Aileen Engel. She hailed from America but we all believed she was British and very Cordon Bleu! She owned a catering business as a side enterprise to flying and I was eager to help in all of her catering gigs, learning, loving and living good food through her. This recipe is an adaptation of an hors d'oeuvre she offered clients who subscribed to her service. Thank you, Aileen, for all the great guidance.

1	olive ficelle	1
8 slices	Italian pancetta or bacon	8
6 oz	soft chèvre (goat cheese)	170 mL
6 oz	cream cheese	170 mL
1 tbsp	creamy horseradish	15 mL
2 tbsp	Dijon mustard	30 mL
$^1/_2$ cup	green pepper, finely diced	120 mL
$^1/_2$ cup	sun-dried tomatoes, finely diced	120 mL
to taste	fresh tellicherry or black pepper	

MAKES 24 SLICES

Cut $^1/_2$ inch (1.2 cm) off both ends of the bread, then cut the bread in half. Carefully remove the soft bread from the center, leaving the crust intact. Set aside.

Coarsely dice the pancetta or bacon. Pan fry until crisp, then transfer to a paper towel to drain any excess fat that remains. Set aside.

Combine the cheeses, horseradish, Dijon mustard, green pepper, sun-dried tomatoes and reserved pancetta or bacon in a mixing bowl. Stir well to combine, adding a good grinding of fresh pepper —I prefer tellicherry.

Place the cheese mixture into a piping bag fitted with a large open tip. Stand the bread on end and squeeze mixture into the hollow. Turn on the opposite end and squeeze in more mixture until the hollowed casing is full of cheese. Pack it down as best you can to avoid any air pockets. Wrap securely in plastic wrap and chill for at least 2 hours. This can be prepared up to 2 days in advance.

To serve, use an electric knife or sharp bread knife and slice the baguette into even slices. Serve cold or at room temperature.

CAREN'S ADVICE

Ficelle is a skinny version of the French baguette. Some are plain, others are olive studded. If ficelle is unavailable where you live, substitute a good quality baguette. Your slices will be a little bit larger in diameter, but certainly no less tasty. If goat cheese is not a favorite, simply double up on the cream cheese.

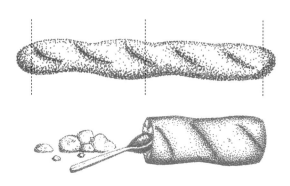

Scalloped Potatoes

Scalloped potatoes, yuck! The name conjures up nasty memories of my childhood when the unthinkable "canned mushroom soup" was married with milk and potatoes in a baked casserole. But my twist on scalloped potatoes is roasted potatoes topped with Asian marinated grilled scallops. This is a version worth trying.

2 tbsp	sesame oil	30 mL
2 tbsp	peanut or grapeseed oil	30 mL
2	large minced garlic cloves	2
1 inch	piece of fresh ginger, finely minced	2.5 cm
1 tbsp	fermented black beans, finely chopped	15 mL
1 tbsp	rice vinegar	15 mL
1 tbsp	hoisin sauce	15 mL
36	fresh bay scallops	36
3	large russet potatoes	3

GARNISH

fresh cilantro leaves

MAKES 36 PIECES

Heat the sesame and peanut or grapeseed oil together, add the garlic, ginger and chopped black beans. Sauté on medium heat until the mixture becomes fragrant, about 3–4 minutes. Add the rice wine vinegar and hoisin. Stir to combine.

When the mixture is cool, add the scallops and let them marinate for at least 30 minutes. Meanwhile, slice the potatoes about $1/8$ inch (.2 cm) thick and, using a 2-inch (5-cm) round cookie cutter, punch out 36 rounds of potato. Brush both sides with oil, place on parchment-lined cookie sheet and bake at 400°F (200°C) for 10 minutes or until they are golden brown and cooked through.

Transfer the potato rounds to a serving platter. When ready to serve, heat a cast iron fry pan or a grill to high, add the scallops and cook for about 3–4 minutes or until cooked through. Place one scallop on each potato slice and garnish with a cilantro leaf.

Mary Ann's Cheese Straws

My friend and long-time student, Mary Ann Horton, gifted me with this recipe. The first time I tasted these cheese straws at her home, she served them in a tall cylindrical cup. I consumed the entire serving alone! Thanks, Mary Ann.

1 cup	sharp cheddar cheese, grated	240 mL
1 cup	unbleached all-purpose flour	240 mL
1 tsp	dry mustard	5 mL
1/4 tsp	smoked paprika, *LA CHINATA*	.5 mL
1 tbsp	butter, melted	15 mL
1/3 cup	milk	80 mL
to taste	sea salt	
to taste	ground tellicherry or black pepper	

MAKES 24 STRAWS

Blend the cheese, flour, dry mustard, smoked paprika, melted butter and milk into a soft dough. Form into a flat disk and refrigerate for about 30 minutes to firm up.

Roll out on a floured board approximately 1/4 inch (1 cm) thick. With a sharp knife or pizza cutter, cut 1/4 x 8 inch strips (1 x 20 cm).

Sprinkle with the sea salt and ground tellicherry pepper. Twist the strips and place on a baking sheet. Bake at 450°F (230°C) for approximately 5 minutes. They should be golden. Do not remove from pan until completely cool.

CAREN'S ADVICE
Substitute the cheese with 1/2 cup (120 mL) black or white sesame seeds, 1/4 cup (60 mL) poppy seeds or 1/4 cup (60 mL) cracked pepper.

La Chinata Smoked Paprika possesses one of those flavors you never forget. A must in your kitchen.

Spicy Thai Appetizer

Don't let the ease of this fool you. Nothing could taste better and provide more palate refreshment than this simple mixture of sugar, salt and chili. Remember—the perfect recipe is the one that can balance sweet, salty, sour and spice in one complete taste.

1 cup	granulated sugar	240 mL
1 tsp	sea salt	5 mL
2–3	chopped jalapeño or serano chilies	2–3
1	jicama, peeled, sliced into thick julienne	1
1 bunch	celery, cut into sticks	1 bunch
2	Granny Smith apples, sliced	2

SERVES 6–8

Mix the sugar, salt and minced chilies together. Place in a small bowl for dipping. Arrange the sliced vegetables and fruit on a serving platter. Place the dipping mixture on the side. Serve with drinks. Great on a hot day!

CAREN'S ADVICE
Jicama is a crunchy sweet turnip/potato-like tuber that has a rough skin. Once peeled, it reveals amazingly juicy flesh that can be used in salads or for dipping.

Hervé Martin, me, José Valagao and Murray Shapiro in the back

Mary Mackay's Pepper Shooters

One often wonders if lengthy, intense preparations make for the best foods. I assure you not. My friend and colleague, Mary Mackay, co-owner/head baker at Terra Breads in Vancouver, created this unbelievably easy, but high-impact taste, appetizer. One of my personal favorites and I know it will rapidly become one of yours. It leaves lots of time for play!

24	pickled sweet or hot cherry peppers, tops removed	24
24	small leaves fresh basil	24
3 oz	provolone cheese, cut into 24 $^3/_4$-inch (2-cm) cubes	85 g
12	very thin slices prosciutto, cut in half	12
2 tbsp	extra virgin olive oil	30 mL

MAKES 2 DOZEN PIECES

Use a small melon baller or teaspoon to scoop the seeds out of the cherry peppers. Discard seeds. Run the peppers under water to rinse out extra seeds and place them upside down on paper towel to drain.

Place one basil leaf on top of each cube of provolone, then wrap a slice of prosciutto around each cube. Stuff the cherry peppers with the prosciutto and provolone packages. Place the stuffed peppers in a bowl and gently toss with the olive oil.

The peppers can be stored in the fridge in a plastic container for your picnic or transferred to a serving dish for immediate consumption.

Truffled Chèvre

The mysterious flavor of truffle combined with chèvre and roasted garlic makes this cheese torte one to brag about.

1 lb	soft goat cheese *WOOLWICH DAIRY*	455 g
1	head roasted garlic, cooled and peeled (see p. 174)	1
3 drops	truffle oil (see p. 27)	
to taste	freshly ground tellicherry or black pepper	
$^1/_2$ cup	white truffle paste	120 mL
1	small baguette or crackers	1
PORT-INFUSED FIGS		
$^1/_3$ cup	port wine	80 mL
1 cup	dried Mission figs, cut into halves	240 mL

SERVES 8–10

Line a narrow 1lb (455 g) terrine with plastic wrap, letting the wrap hang over the edges.

Mix the chèvre with the peeled roasted garlic, add a few drops of the truffle oil and a good grinding of the pepper. Mix well.

Spread half the cheese into the prepared terrine pan, then spread the truffle paste evenly over. Top with the remaining cheese. Fold over the overlapping plastic wrap, pressing down to eliminate any air pockets. Chill for at least 2 hours.

PORT-INFUSED FIGS
Heat the port to a low simmer, add the figs, turn off the heat and let the port infuse the figs. Cool and serve with the cheese and baguette or crackers.

Bruschetta Rustica

This is undoubtedly the best way to use up day-old bread. I prefer the crusty rustic breads that dominate the cottage bakeries of late. I also prefer an unfiltered extra virgin olive oil like Tenuta del Numerouno or Calvi. This is, without a doubt, a hold-me-back recipe! A reason to save and covet stale bread.

1	loaf stale French or Italian bread	1
2–3	large garlic cloves, peeled and cut in half	2–3
	extra virgin olive oil, *TENUTA DEL NUMEROUNO* or *CALVI*	
	fleur de sel	
	freshly ground tellicherry or black pepper	

SERVES 6

Slice the bread into about $1/2$-inch (1.2-cm) rounds, and broil it on both sides until it is golden but not dark brown. Rub the toasted bread on both sides with the garlic cloves. Generously drizzle the bread with the olive oil on both sides, making sure that it is evenly anointed. Lightly sprinkle with fleur de sel and ground tellicherry pepper. Perfect with salad.

One Dozen Eggs

This is a remake of the very popular but worn appetizer of the 50s. It seemed there wasn't a potluck where these stuffed eggs didn't make an appearance. Fortunately, they faded away with time. Fast forward 50 years, to new flavor definitions and a very savvy presentation. Ditch the frilly bib apron and don those fishnet stockings!

6	hard-boiled eggs	6
$1/4$ cup	mayonnaise, *HELLMAN'S*	60 mL
1 tbsp	Dijon mustard	15 mL
1 tsp	capers	5 mL
2–3 tbsp	fresh cilantro, minced	30–45 mL
1 tsp	smoked paprika, *LA CHINATA*	5 mL
to taste	sea salt and cracked pepper	
1	anchovy fillet, minced (optional)	1
to taste	piri piri sauce (see p. 54)	

GARNISH

cilantro sprigs

small niçoise olives, *ARNAUD*

MAKES 12 PIECES

Cut the eggs in half as shown. Scoop out the yolks, place them in a bowl and mash well with a fork. Add the mayonnaise, mustard, capers, cilantro, paprika, salt and pepper, anchovy if desired, and piri piri sauce. Adjust seasoning to taste.

Spoon or pipe the filling into the egg halves. Garnish with the niçoise olives and a sprig of cilantro. Pack into an empty egg carton. If they are a little loose, stuff some plastic wrap in the bottom to secure. Let chill for at least 30 minutes before serving.

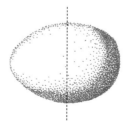

Candied Salmon Pâté

I like to use Westcoast Select's candied salmon—their secret ingredient always makes my recipe development a breeze! This is as simple as it gets, with outstanding results. My thanks to Dave and all the good guys over at Westcoast Select Salmon, you have one hellava good product! Remember, if you can't get their product, simply use regular sliced smoked salmon.

1 (8 oz)	pkg candied salmon or regular sliced smoked salmon, *WESTCOAST SELECT*	1 (240 g)
10 oz	cream cheese	284 mL
2 tbsp	creamy horseradish (hot)	30 mL
1/2	fresh lime, juiced	1/2
1	small shallot, finely diced	1
1/4 cup	fresh dill	60 mL
	pumpernickel rounds, cucumber slices or daikon radish slices	

GARNISH

fresh dill sprigs

fried capers

MAKES 48 PIECES

Skin the salmon, break up into pieces and place in the bowl of a Cuisinart. Pulse the machine until it breaks up the salmon. Add the cream cheese, horseradish, lime juice, shallot and dill. Run the machine until the mixture is smooth and creamy. Place the mixture into a piping bag fitted with a large star tip, pipe onto pumpernickel rounds, cucumber slices or daikon radish slices. Garnish with a sprig of fresh dill and a few of the fried capers.

CAREN'S ADVICE

To fry capers, pour grapeseed or peanut oil to a level of 1/2 inch (1 cm) in a small pan and heat. Blot capers and dry very well. Fry one tablespoon at a time in the hot oil. Drain on paper towels. Use as a garnish for salads, fish or hors d'oeuvres.

Pissaladière

Pissaladière is the darling of the French Riviera, calling Nice its home and boasting the flavors of all that is fabulous in the south of France. This is great as a light lunch or cut into small squares as an appetizer.

DOUGH

1 tsp	sugar	5 mL
1/2 cup	warm water	120 mL
1 tbsp	yeast	15 mL
3 cups	unbleached all-purpose flour	720 mL
1 tsp	sea salt	5 mL
2	large eggs, lightly beaten	2
1/2 cup	milk	120 mL

FILLING

1/4 cup	olive oil	60 mL
5	Spanish onions, sliced	5
2	garlic cloves, minced	2
1/2 tsp	dried thyme leaves	2.5 mL
1/4 cup	milk	60 mL
2 oz	can anchovies	57 g
1 tsp	freshly ground tellicherry or black pepper	5 mL
1/2 cup	freshly grated Parmesan	120 mL
14	kalamata olives	14

SERVES 6–8

DOUGH

Dissolve the sugar in water, sprinkle the yeast over top. Let it sit until it begins to bubble, about 5–8 minutes. Place the flour and salt in the bowl of a Cuisinart. Add lightly beaten eggs, milk and proofed yeast. Pulse the machine 5 times, then let it run until the dough forms a ball. Turn out onto a lightly floured board and knead until smooth and elastic. Place into a lightly oiled bowl, making sure that the surface of the dough is oiled. Let it rise until double in size, about 1 hour.

FILLING

Heat the olive oil in a large fry pan. Add the onions and fry on medium heat for 10 minutes. Add the garlic and fry for about 5 minutes until golden brown. Add the thyme and stir. Set aside when cooked.

While the onions are cooking, place the milk in a shallow saucer. Drain the anchovies and place them in the milk. This will remove most of the saltiness from the anchovies. Let them sit in the milk for about 15 minutes. Blot dry on paper towels and then cut them in half lengthwise. Set aside.

When the dough has doubled, spread it into an oiled 12 x 17 inch (30 x 43 cm) sided cookie sheet, making sure you push the dough right to the edges. Spread the cooled onions evenly on top of the dough. Take the reserved anchovies and create a diamond pattern on top of the onions. Place an olive inside each of the squares. Sprinkle with the Parmesan cheese. Let the pissaladière rise for 45 minutes. If you prefer a thinner crust, reduce the rising time to 30 minutes.

Bake at 425°F (215°C) for 40 minutes.

Prosciutto and Provolone Wonton

I like to keep packages of wonton wrappers on hand for quick appetizers. Unlike filo pastry, this is really a no-brainer because it doesn't dry out.

24	square wonton wrappers	24
	extra virgin olive oil for brushing wonton	
8 oz	provolone cheese	225 mL
12	thin slices of prosciutto di Parma	12
3 tbsp	truffle honey (see p. 27)	45 mL

MAKES 24

Preheat the oven to 325°F (165°C).

Lightly brush the wonton wrappers on both sides with oil. Be frugal with the oil. You want just enough to make the wrapper glisten, not deep fry it. Carefully press the wrapper against the muffin form in a mini muffin baking pan, so the cup stays open and doesn't collapse inward. Bake for 8–10 minutes or until light golden brown. Do not over-bake. Set aside until serving.

Cut the cheese into $1/2$-inch (1.2-cm) cubes. Lay the prosciutto on your work surface, cut in half lengthwise. Place a cheese cube at the end of a prosciutto slice, then roll up. Place in the wonton cup and bake at 300°F (150°C) for 5–8 minutes or until the cheese has melted.

Remove from oven, transfer to a serving platter and drizzle the tops of each cup with the truffle honey.

Black Bean Chicken

Black bean sauce has long been the darling of Chinese food. Commonly paired with prawns, the sauce has never met a doggy bag. This chicken is an outstanding appetizer and could also stand solo as a main course.

3	large chicken breasts, boneless, skinless	3
3	large garlic cloves	3
2 inch	piece fresh ginger, peeled and finely minced	5 cm
5 tbsp	fermented black beans	75 mL
1/2 cup	grapeseed or peanut oil	120 mL
1/4 cup	soy sauce	60 mL
1 tsp	sugar	5 mL

SERVES 6

Rinse and pat the chicken dry on paper towels. Set aside. Mince the garlic and ginger and coarsely chop the black beans. Place beans in a bowl with the garlic and ginger. Stir in the oil, soy sauce and sugar, mixing well to combine.

Spread the chicken on both sides with the black bean mix. Grill or fry on medium heat until cooked through, about 5–8 minutes.

At this point, you can cut the chicken into bite-sized pieces and skewer it for an appetizer or leave it whole for a main course. Rice works well as a side dish to calm the saltiness of the black beans.

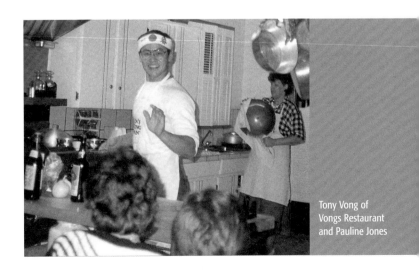

Tony Vong of Vongs Restaurant and Pauline Jones

Mini Artichokes and Bresaola

Two great ingredients: artichokes and bresaola. I like to use the tiny jarred artichokes from Orto Conserviera. If you can't locate them, use regular artichokes and cut them into quarters. Bresaola is a wonderful air-dried beef that is produced largely in Switzerland. Alternatives are dry-cured salami or prosciutto.

1	loaf sliced white sandwich bread	1
	olive oil for brushing the bread	
1 (8 oz)	jar of mini artichokes *ORTO CONSERVIERA*	1 (280 g)
12	thin slices bresaola or quality salami	12

AVOCADO BUTTER

1	avocado	1
1	garlic clove, minced	1
3	sun-dried tomatoes, soaked and minced	3
1/2	fresh lime, juice of	1/2
2 tsp	Dijon mustard	10 mL
to taste	sea salt	
to taste	ground black pepper	

GARNISH

fresh chives or other small herb

MAKES 24 PIECES

Preheat the oven to 375°F (190°C). Cut the crusts from the bread. Using a rolling pin, roll the bread slices out quite thin. Cut circles from the bread using a round or fluted cutter that is 1/4 inch (1 cm) larger in diameter than the pan openings. Brush the bread lightly on both sides with olive oil. Gently press the bread circles into a mini tartlet pan and bake for about 10 minutes, or until the bread cases are golden brown. Cool and set aside.

To prepare the avocado butter, place all the ingredients in a Cuisinart and purée or, alternatively, mash the avocado until it is smooth and add to the remaining ingredients, stirring until you have a smooth butter.

To assemble, place a heaping teaspoon of the butter in the bottom of the bread case, cut the slice of bresaola in half lengthwise, roll it up to resemble a rose, leaving the center open, and place the mini artichoke in the center. Garnish with a chive or small fresh herb stem.

CAREN'S ADVICE

When I first saw these mini artichokes, I could not believe how incredibly perfect they were. Hand picked and peeled, they are fabulous.

Harissa Prawns

Harissa is a very spicy condiment with its roots imbedded in Moroccan cuisine. If spice does not light up your life, use a scant teaspoon. Preserved lemon is also a common ingredient in Moroccan cooking. They both add a flavor dimension that is like no other. Try it, you'll love it!

2 tbsp	olive oil	30 mL
2	large shallots	2
2	garlic cloves, minced	2
1 inch	fresh ginger, peeled and minced	2.5 cm
2 tsp	anchovy paste	10 mL
1 tbsp	smoked paprika, *LA CHINATA*	15 mL
2 tbsp	prepared harissa (see p. 17)	30 mL
2	whole tomatoes, peeled and seeded	2
¼ cup	white wine	60 mL
to taste	sea salt	
2 tbsp	preserved lemon, chopped (see p. 23)	30 mL
	or	
2 tsp	lemon rind, grated	10 mL
24	large prawns (see p. 118)	24

MAKES 24 PIECES

Heat the oil in a medium sauté pan. Add the shallots, garlic, ginger and anchovy paste, sautéing until fragrant and soft, but not brown. Add the paprika, harissa, tomatoes, white wine, sea salt and preserved lemon or lemon rind. Continue to simmer until the sauce thickens. Taste for seasoning and let cool.

Peel the prawns, leaving the tail intact. When the sauce is cool, rub it over the prawns on all sides to coat well. Heat your grill or fry pan to high heat and brush with a little oil. Add the prawns in a single layer, turning only once. As soon as they turn pink, remove from the pan, skewer with a fancy bamboo pick and serve warm or at room temperature.

The cooking school team at work: Susan Meister, Clara McSherry, Amarilde Lourença, Doreen Corday and me

Grilled Calamari

If smoky spice is not the power you want packed into your sauce, cut the chilies to one only. This sauce also works very well with chicken or even scallops.

1–2	chipotle chilies in adobo	1–2
2 tbsp	grapeseed oil	30 mL
1 cup	tomato sauce	240 mL
3 tbsp	corn syrup	45 mL
3	garlic cloves, minced	3
2	shallots, minced	2
2 tbsp	balsamic vinegar	30 mL
1 tsp	orange zest	5 mL
4 tbsp	ketjap manis	60 mL
18	cleaned calamari	18

SERVES 6–8

Finely chop the chipotle chili(s). Heat the grapeseed oil in a pot and add the tomato sauce, chili(s), corn syrup, garlic, shallots, vinegar, orange zest and ketjap manis. Simmer on low heat until the ingredients are blended. Flatten the calamari out on your work surface. Double skewer the calamari and lay in shallow pan. Pour the marinade over top. Chill until serving. This can be done a day ahead.

Heat the barbecue or grill to medium high heat. Lay the skewered calamari on the grill and cook on both sides for about 3 minutes each side. Serve hot off the grill or at room temperature.

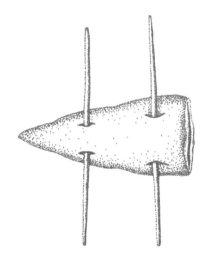

CAREN'S ADVICE
Chipotle chilies are in fact smoked jalapeño peppers packed in a spicy sauce called adobo.

Asparagus, Goat Cheese and Salmon Terrine

This terrine is made special with an Indian candied salmon, produced in Vancouver by a company called Westcoast Select. Don't fret if you are not a local and can't get it, simply substitute regular sliced smoked salmon. Either way you will be a winner.

12–15	fresh asparagus spears	12–15
12 oz	goat cheese	340 mL
4	sliced shallots, fried crisp and drained on paper towel	4
2 tbsp	Dijon mustard	30 mL
2 tbsp	horseradish	30 mL
to taste	fresh ground black pepper	
1/2 lb	smoked Indian candy, skin removed, and flaked, WESTCOAST SELECT	225 g
1/2 cup	fresh dill sprigs	120 mL

SERVES 6–8

Line a 3-cup (720 mL) terrine mold with plastic wrap, allowing 2 inches (5 cm) to hang over the edge. Blanch the asparagus in boiling water for about 2 minutes, refresh in cold water. Drain, slice the spears in half lengthwise and set aside.

Mix the goat cheese with the shallots, mustard and horseradish and add the pepper to taste. Press a layer of the goat cheese mixture in the bottom of the terrine. Lay the asparagus on top in a single layer, then a layer of salmon, and finally the fresh dill. Repeat this layering until you have used all the product. Wrap over the overhang of plastic to enclose the terrine. Press down to compress the terrine, chill for at least 2 hours.

This can be served as a terrine on a buffet or sliced and placed on a bed of greens as a first course.

West Coast Crab Cakes

Crab cakes are the darling of every cocktail party. What separates good from bad? Crab! Please, never substitute imitation crab meat, always use Dungeness and plenty of it! If not, you simply have a potato cake. These taste good with a crowning of Garlic Aïoli (see p. 96).

1	large russet potato, cooked, peeled and grated	1
1	large egg, beaten	1
2 tbsp	mayonnaise	30 mL
1 1/2 tbsp	Dijon mustard	20 mL
1	green onion, finely chopped	1
2 tbsp	fresh chives, chopped	30 mL
1/4 cup	fresh red pepper, diced	60 mL
1 tsp	piri piri sauce	5 mL
to taste	sea salt	
to taste	freshly ground tellicherry or black pepper	
3/4 lb	fresh Dungeness crab meat	340 g
1 cup	toasted ground hazelnuts	240 mL
	unsalted butter and peanut oil in equal portions for frying	

MAKES 24 PIECES

In a large bowl, combine the grated potato, beaten egg, mayonnaise, mustard, onion, chives, red pepper, piri piri sauce, salt and pepper. Mix to incorporate the ingredients. Mix in the crab meat and adjust the seasonings. Form the mixture into patties and roll the edges in the toasted ground hazelnuts. Press the nuts in firmly so they stick.

Heat a frying pan to medium, add equal portions of butter and oil, about 1 tbsp (15 mL) of each to start. Fry the cakes on both sides until golden brown, about 1–2 minutes each side. Serve warm.

CAREN'S ADVICE

Piri piri peppers are native to Africa. The Portuguese brought the peppers home and created a fermented hot sauce aptly named "piri piri."

Curry Chicken Wonton

Wonton wrappers are the darling of the appetizer world because they are so easy to work with. They are very cost-effective and provide a light, calorie-conscious base for your filling. Lack of imagination is the only thing holding you back.

12	square wonton wrappers	12
	flavorless oil for brushing (e.g. grapeseed)	
1 tbsp	butter	15 mL
2	large shallots, diced	2
2	minced garlic cloves	2
1 inch	piece fresh ginger, grated	2.5 cm
1 lb	chicken breast, boned and skinned	455 g
3 tbsp	packaged curry paste, or more to taste	45 mL
½–¾ cup	coconut milk	120–180 mL
⅓ cup	prepared chutney, *MAJOR GREY*	80 mL
squeeze	lemon juice	
to taste	sea salt	

GARNISH

fresh cilantro

black sesame seeds

MAKES 48 PIECES

Preheat the oven to 325°F (175°C). Cut the wonton wrappers into quarters, lightly brushing each side with oil. Press into mini muffin cups and bake for about 5 minutes, or until golden brown. Let cool.

Melt the butter in a sauté pan, add the shallots, garlic and ginger and sauté until fragrant, but not brown. Dice the chicken into ¼-inch (.6-cm) pieces. Add to the pan and cook for about 5 minutes. Add the curry paste, coconut milk, chutney and lemon juice. Continue to cook until the chicken is done and the sauce is thick. Adjust the seasoning with sea salt and more curry paste if desired. At this point the dish can be chilled until ready to serve.

When ready to serve, reheat the curry mixture, spoon into the prepared wontons, garnish with the cilantro and a sprinkle of sesame seeds.

A nice serving option is to place the wonton in steamer baskets that are lined with banana leaves, available in Asian markets.

Jack Stoughton,
Lois Gilbert,
Susan Meister,
John Ash,
Ruth Grierson,
Hugh Carpenter,
Cindy Burridge,
Kerry Sear,
Pauline Jones,
Doreen Corday, and
David Osachoff

California Sushi Rolls

Once the rice is made, these sushi rolls are a breeze to make. You too can be a sushi chef wanna-be!

SUSHI RICE

3 1/3 cups	short grain rice (Japanese sticky rice)	800 mL
4 cups	water	950 mL

RICE DRESSING

5 tbsp	rice vinegar	75 mL
5 tbsp	sugar	75 mL
4 tsp	sea salt	20 mL

FILLING

6	nori sheets	6
1	English cucumber, cut into 1/2 x 5 inch (1 x 12.5 cm) sticks	1
2	avocados	2
1 cup	sprouts, alfalfa or sunflower	240 mL
1 cup	sesame seeds	240 mL
4 oz	smoked salmon	100 g
	caviar or tobiko (optional)	
to taste	wasabi	
1/2 cup	pickled ginger	120 mL

MAKES 36 PIECES

Place the rice and water in a rice cooker. Let it cook. Meanwhile, place the vinegar, sugar and salt in a small pot. Cook on medium heat just to dissolve the sugar. Cool. When the rice is cooked place it in a shallow pan. Pour the vinegar dressing over top and mix, being careful not to mush the rice up. Fan off the steam so you do not get soggy rice. Cool to room temperature and cover with a damp kitchen towel until ready to use.

ASSEMBLY

Lay the nori on a bamboo mat, dampen your hands with water and scoop up some rice, and smooth it evenly over half of the nori. Arrange the assorted fillings in a row near the edge of the nori. Do not choose them all for one roll, make an assortment. Dampen the edge of the nori with water or rice vinegar. Take your bamboo mat and firmly roll and pull on the nori making a snug tight sushi roll.

Set aside until all are completed. Using a very sharp knife cut clean through the rolls. These can be assembled early and kept chilled. Wrap securely with plastic film to prevent drying.

Mix the wasabi according to package directions and serve alongside the sushi together with the pickled ginger.

Santa Fe Chicken

My dear friend Bob Lawrence has made this so many times that he has it memorized. A quick dish you never tire of, it works equally well as an appetizer served with corn chips or as a main course wrapped with warmed flour tortillas and a seasoned rice.

½ cup	olive oil	120 mL
1 cup	yellow onion, diced	240 mL
4	garlic cloves, minced	4
2	red bell peppers, seeded and diced	2
1 (14 oz)	can kernel corn, drained	1 (398 mL)
3	chicken breasts boneless, skinned and cut into bite-size pieces	3
2–3 tbsp	hot chili powder	30–45 mL
1 tsp	ground cumin	5 mL
½	bunch cilantro, chopped	½
1 tsp	hot pepper flakes (optional)	5 mL
1 pkg	8-inch (20-cm) flour tortillas, or 1 bag corn chips	1 pkg
1 cup	sour cream	240 mL

SERVES 6

Heat ¼ cup (60 mL) of the oil in a wide sauté pan. When the oil is hot, add the onion and 2 of the garlic cloves. Cook for about 5 minutes or until softened, but not brown. Add the red peppers and corn and cook over medium heat for 5 more minutes or until vegetables are soft. Remove and set aside.

In the same pan, heat the remaining ¼ cup (60 mL) of oil. When the oil is hot, add the 2 remaining garlic cloves along with the chicken. Cook, turning occasionally, for about 10 minutes or until well browned. Stir in the chili, cumin, cilantro and hot pepper flakes if using.

Add the reserved pepper and corn mixture and heat through to blend the flavors. Taste and season with salt. Serve on a decorative platter with wedges of warm flour tortillas or corn chips, and sour cream.

Ruy Paes-Braga and me

Sesame Chicken Strips

The addition of sesame seeds gives this chicken an interesting crunch and it beats the hell out of boxed chicken fingers!

1	garlic clove, minced	1
1	large egg	1
1 tbsp	soy sauce	15 mL
1 inch	piece fresh ginger, grated or rasped	2.5 cm
2 tbsp	sherry or port	30 mL
1 tbsp	lemon rind, grated or rasped	15 mL
to taste	fresh ground tellicherry or black pepper	
1 lb	chicken breast, boned and skinned, cut into strips	455 g
2 cups	peanut or grapeseed oil	480 mL

COATING

³/₄ cup	white sesame seeds	180 mL
³/₄ cup	black sesame seeds	180 mL
¹/₃ cup	cornstarch	80 mL

SERVES 4–6

APRICOT SAUCE

8 oz	jar plum or apricot jam	230 g
1 tbsp	grainy mustard	15 mL
1 tbsp	balsamic vinegar	15 mL
1 tsp	grated lemon rind or preserved lemon (see p. 23)	5 mL

MAKES 1 CUP (240 ML)

Combine the garlic, egg, soy sauce, ginger, sherry or port, lemon rind and pepper and mix well. Place the chicken in a large zip-lock bag and pour the marinade in. Seal and refrigerate for at least two hours. Overnight is best.

Combine the white and black sesame seeds and stir in the cornstarch. Place in a shallow saucer. Set aside.

In a heavy-bottomed shallow pan, heat oil to high. Dip the chicken pieces in the sesame mixture and drop into the hot oil. The chicken will sizzle and brown immediately. Cook on both sides for about 1 minute each. Remove and blot on paper towels to remove any excess oil. Serve with apricot sauce.

APRICOT SAUCE
Place all the ingredients in a small pot and heat through, taking time to break up any fruit that is in chunks. Serve alongside the chicken as a dip or side sauce.

Prosciutto-Wrapped Prawns
with Basil Dipping Sauce

Every time I make this appetizer it brings back a vivid memory of Crystal Cruises. I was very fortunate to be invited on several occasions to be a guest chef with Crystal. As is their policy, the guest chef's dinner is held on Saturday evening. It is given a focus on the menu, but I was assured that never more than 30% of diners choose this menu. Together with the Executive Chef, we calculated the numbers and prepped accordingly. The first sitting began in normal fashion, but within 20 minutes we found ourselves doing second and third helpings. Some people requested the prawns as their main course. Needless to say, we exhausted every single prawn we had prepped for the second seating. Flattered and sweating profusely, I never dreamed we would be wrapping close to 1,700 prawns in one day. So whatever your thoughts are regarding numbers, double them—they go as fast as M&M's at a birthday party!

2	large shallots, roasted	2
2 cups	firmly packed fresh basil leaves	480 mL
2–3	peeled garlic cloves	2–3
3 tbsp	pine nuts	45 mL
2 tsp	balsamic vinegar	10 mL
1/2 cup	extra virgin olive oil	120 mL
to taste	sea salt	
to taste	tellicherry pepper or black pepper	
18	large prawns, head off, tail on	18
9	thin slices of prosciutto, preferably Italian	9

MAKES 18 PIECES

To roast the shallots, peel and rub lightly with olive oil. Place them in a garlic roaster or wrap in foil and bake at 325°F (165°C) for about 40 minutes, or until they are soft and golden in color.

Place the roasted shallots, basil, garlic, pine nuts and vinegar in a blender or Cuisinart and purée until the mixture is smooth, scraping down the sides of the bowl once or twice. With the motor running, slowly pour in the olive oil. The sauce will thicken slightly. Season with the sea salt and the tellicherry pepper.

Dry prawns thoroughly. Cut the prosciutto in half lengthwise and wrap one piece around the body of each prawn. Rub the wrapped prawn with a scant amount of olive oil. Heat a barbecue or grill to high. Cook the prawns until they are bright pink, turning only once. This should take about 3–4 minutes. Serve hot off the grill with the basil sauce.

CAREN'S ADVICE

In a pinch for time? Use a jar of pesto sauce thinned down with 3 tbsp (45 mL) extra virgin olive oil for the dip. I like to use Italia Intavola. Let's face it, Italy was first to bring the world Pesto Genovse.

Filo Pizza

The perfect appetizer to begin a meal! Filo is ideal for light eating. You can substitute any topping, but keep in mind that filo is very thin, so do not overload the top or you will wear through the bottom!

6–8	sheets filo pastry	6–8
	olive oil for brushing filo dough	
1/2 cup	freshly grated Parmesan	120 mL
1 cup	grated mozzarella or Swiss cheese	240 mL
1 cup	sliced sweet onion	240 mL
5	Roma tomatoes, sliced	5
1 tsp	dried oregano	5 mL
1 tsp	dried thyme	5 mL
to taste	fresh ground pepper	

GARNISH

1/3 cup	finely chopped parsley	80 mL

SERVES 6–8

Preheat the oven to 375°F (190°C). To make the base, lightly oil an 11 x 8 inch (27.5 x 20 cm) cookie sheet, lay a sheet of filo on top, lightly brush with oil, sprinkle a tablespoon of Parmesan over top and gently press so that they stick together. Repeat, using all the sheets of filo to create a base.

Sprinkle the top of the pizza with the mozzarella or Swiss cheese, then the sliced onion. Lay the tomatoes on top. Finish with an even sprinkle of the herbs and pepper. Bake for 20–25 minutes or until the edges are golden brown. Garnish with parsley.

Cut into squares and serve hot.

News, Weather and Sports hamming it up: Mark Madryga, Jill Krop and Steve Darling

Nana's Rice Paper Rolls
with Dipping Sauce

3 tbsp	grapeseed oil	45 mL
2	shallots, minced	2
1	large garlic clove, minced	1
1 cup	fresh shiitake mushrooms, sliced	240 mL
1 cup	white button mushrooms, sliced	240 mL
2 tbsp	fresh ginger, minced	30 mL
3	medium carrots, grated	3
3/4 cup	sweet onion, sliced thin	180 mL
1 cup	red pepper, julienned	240 mL
1 cup	water chestnuts, sliced	240 mL
1/3 cup	fresh cilantro, chopped	80 mL
1/3 cup	fresh parsley, chopped	80 mL
1/4 cup	fresh mint, chopped	60 mL
2 cups	cooked chicken meat, shredded, or cooked shrimp meat	480 mL
to taste	sea salt	
to taste	fresh ground pepper	
1 (1 lb)	pkg of rice paper 8 inch (20 cm) rounds	1 (454 g)
2–3 tbsp	grapeseed oil for frying	30–45 mL

MAKES 24–30 ROLLS

DIPPING SAUCE

1 tbsp	grapeseed oil	15 mL
3	green onions, sliced thin	3
2 tbsp	fresh ginger, minced	30 mL
2 tbsp	chili paste	30 mL
1 tbsp	hoisin sauce	15 mL
1 tbsp	soy sauce	15 mL
1 tbsp	sugar	15 mL
2 tbsp	rice vinegar	30 mL
1 tbsp	fish sauce	15 mL
3 tbsp	sesame oil	45 mL

MAKES 1/2 CUP (120 ML)

My wonderful nanny, Elizabeth Flores, who has been with me for the past 13 years, often cooks with me. She has a great sense for South East Asian flavors, and together we worked this spring roll into an irresistible, can't-stop first course.

Heat the oil in a large fry pan, add the shallots and garlic. Cook until softened but do not brown. Add both cups of mushrooms to the pan and sauté for about 5 minutes, or until they begin to soften and release liquid. Add the ginger, carrots, onion, red pepper, water chestnuts and herbs to the pan. With the heat on high, fry this mixture for a few minutes, just until the moisture of the vegetables has gone. Add the cooked chicken or shrimp, stirring to combine, and season with salt and pepper. Let cool while you make the dipping sauce.

In a small stainless steel saucepan, heat the oil. Add the green onions, ginger and chili paste. Cook on low heat just until the onions are soft but not browned. Remove from the heat and add all the remaining ingredients, stirring to combine well. Cool and serve alongside the rolls.

To assemble the rolls, place the rice paper rounds, 6 at a time, in a shallow pan of warm water—just long enough to soften them. The papers will become soft and pliable. Blot them lightly on cotton tea towels. Lay the rice paper on your work surface and spoon a generous tablespoon of filling on top. Fold the sides over, then roll up jelly roll fashion. Set aside and repeat using all the filling. If smaller rolls are desired, purchase smaller rice papers. Heat 2–3 tbsp (30–45 mL) grapeseed oil in a large nonstick pan. Fry the rolls on all sides until golden brown. Serve hot or at room temperature with the dipping sauce.

soups, salads & first courses

Gin and Tomato Soup

The very first time I prepared this soup was for my friend Chef Pierre Dubrulle. He had hired me to teach in his school, so I invited him and some friends to dinner. Being young and new to teaching, I was extremely nervous about cooking for this well-known chef. As the evening progressed the wine flowed, my nerves calmed, and consequently, I didn't pay attention to the temperature of the soup when I added the cream. Disaster struck on the first course. The soup curdled and I died! What to do? With no back up, I turned the lights out, candles only and prayed that no one would notice the overkill of garnish hiding the curdles of cream. Because a curdle of cream does not alter the taste of the soup, I served it to rave reviews, never fessing up to what went wrong. The moral of the story? Never apologize for what you serve your guests. How it turns out is the way you wanted it! Well, except for curdled soup!

8	ripe tomatoes, peeled and seeded	8
2 cups	vegetable or beef stock	480 mL
3	garlic cloves, minced	3
1 tsp	thyme	5 mL
4	pancetta strips, diced and fried crisp	4
1/3 cup	sour cream	80 mL
2 cups	table cream	480 mL
1/3 cup	gin	80 mL
to taste	sea salt	
to taste	freshly ground black pepper	
1/2 tsp	piri piri sauce (see p. 54)	2.5 mL

SERVES 4–6

Purée the tomatoes, stock, garlic cloves and thyme using a Cuisinart. Place in a saucepan and bring to a boil. Combine the pancetta and sour cream, setting aside for garnish. Add the table cream to the soup base but make sure the soup is not too hot or the cream will curdle. Add the gin and the seasonings, ladle into warmed bowls and garnish with the bacon mixture and a dash of piri piri.

CAREN'S ADVICE: PEELING TOMATOES

Place the tomatoes in a pot of just-boiled water. Count to 10 and remove them with a slotted spoon. The skin will have split. Simply slip the skin away from the flesh. Cut the tomato in half and squeeze out the seeds.

Pierre Dubrulle and Pauline Jones

Roasted Garlic and Spinach Soup

Soup in 20 minutes puts this recipe on top of cooking on the run. Two advantages: quick as well as not too filling, it can double as a starter for dinner or make a perfect lunch with some Fig and Shallot Focaccia (see p. 126).

3 tbsp	extra virgin olive oil	45 mL
1 large	onion, diced	1
2	leeks, cleaned and diced	2
5–6	large Roma tomatoes, diced	5–6
8 cups	chicken or vegetable stock	2 L
2 cups	small, shaped dried pasta	480 mL
1 tsp	dried oregano	5 mL
1 tsp	dried thyme	5 mL
2	bunches fresh spinach leaves, stemmed and washed	2
2	heads roasted garlic, (see p. 174) cooled and peeled	2
to taste	sea salt	
to taste	freshly ground tellicherry or black pepper	

GARNISH

	fresh grated Parmesan cheese	
1 cup	fresh basil leaves, cut into chiffonade	240 mL

SERVES 6

Heat the oil in a soup pot, add the onion and leeks and sauté until soft and lightly golden brown. Add the diced tomatoes and cook for about 2 minutes. Stir in the stock and bring to a boil. Once the stock has boiled add the pasta, oregano and thyme. Cook just until the pasta is almost cooked, 10–12 minutes. Coarsely chop the spinach and add to the pot along with the peeled cloves of roasted garlic, sea salt and pepper.

Once the pasta is cooked through and the spinach is soft, ladle into bowls, top with the basil and generous spoons of Parmesan.

CAREN'S ADVICE: CHIFFONADE

A simple technique to shred leafy vegetables and herbs. Simply stack the leaves flat and then roll them into a tight cylinder and slice finely. The result will be fine shreds called chiffonade.

Parisian Four Onion Soup

Onion Soup ranks as a menu favorite everywhere. I have had my share of weak, watery versions where even one lonely onion was difficult to find. The stock should be a rich amber color, full of dark caramelized onions and oozing with a Swiss Gruyère gratin as a crowning finish. This recipe has it all. If one or more of the onions is unavailable, double up on what you can find.

1/2 cup	unsalted butter (see p. 13)	120 mL
2 cups	Bermuda onion, sliced approx. 1 large (purple)	480 mL
2 cups	Spanish onion, sliced approx. 1 large	480 mL
2 cups	white sweet onion, sliced approx. 1 large	480 mL
2 cups	yellow onion, sliced approx. 1 large	480 mL
2 tbsp	sugar	30 mL
4–6	garlic cloves, minced	4–6
8 cups	chicken or beef stock	2 L
1	bay leaf	1
2 tbsp	cracked pepper	30 mL
2 tsp	thyme	10 mL
2 tbsp	Dijon mustard	30 mL
1 tbsp	freshly ground tellicherry or black pepper	15 mL
6–8	toasted French bread slices, rubbed with cut garlic clove (optional)	6–8
1/2 cup	white wine	120 mL
1/3 cup	brandy	80 mL
2 cups	Swiss Gruyère cheese, grated	480 mL
1 cup	fresh Parmesan, grated	240 mL

SERVES 6–8

Melt the butter in a large soup pot, add the sliced onions and cook for 10 minutes on medium to high heat. Sprinkle in the sugar and continue to cook until well caramelized. Add the garlic and cook two more minutes. Add the stock, bay leaf, cracked pepper, thyme, mustard and ground pepper. Simmer for about 30 minutes.

Cut the French bread into 1/2-inch (1-cm) slices, and toast in a slow oven until well dried out. Rub the bread with a cut garlic clove if desired. Set aside.

About 10 minutes before serving the soup, add the wine and brandy. Adjust the pepper to taste. Ladle the soup into oven-proof bowls and place a toasted bread slice on top. Sprinkle generously with the Swiss cheese and then a little Parmesan. Broil until bubbly and brown.

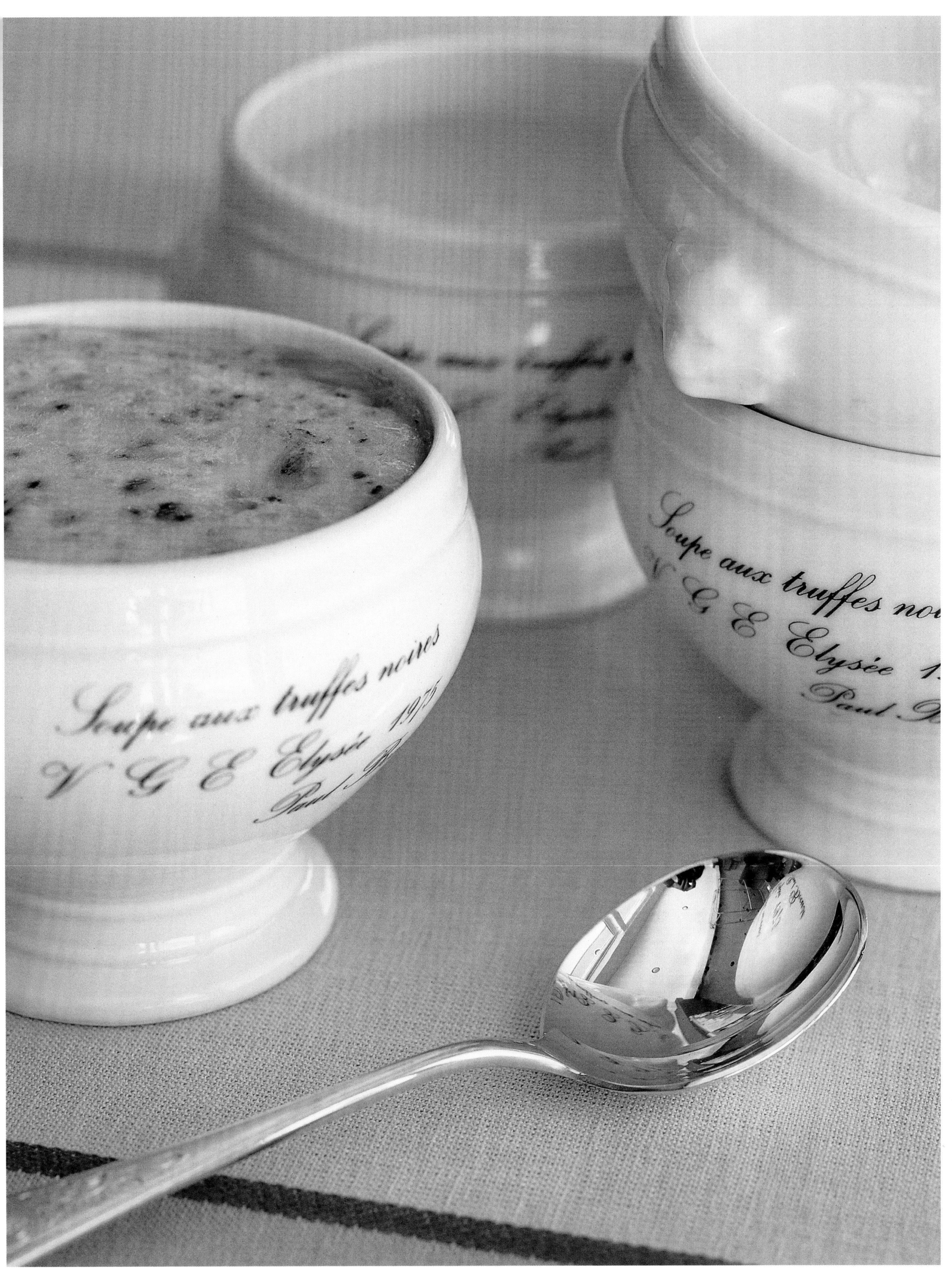
Soupe aux truffes noires
V G E Elysée 1975

Ribollita

A very old-fashioned Tuscan-style bread and vegetable soup. A perfect meal date for those frosty winter nights when comfort and food are your best friends.

2 cups	white navy beans	480 mL
2–3 tbsp	olive oil	30–45 mL
1	large yellow onion, diced	1
3	large garlic cloves, minced	3
1	large carrot, diced	1
1	medium zucchini, diced	1
2	celery stalks, diced	2
1/2	head sui choy/Napa cabbage, shredded	1/2
4 tbsp	tomato paste	60 mL
1	large bunch fresh spinach, cleaned and stemmed	1
3 cups	chicken stock	720 mL
1	bunch fresh basil, chopped	1
to taste	sea salt	
to taste	freshly ground pepper	
1	large loaf day old crusty bread, cubed	1

GARNISH

5 oz	spicy pancetta, fried crispy	150 g
	Parmesan cheese, freshly grated	
1/2	bunch Italian parsley, chopped	1/2
	unfiltered estate olive oil	

SERVES 6–8

Cover the beans with cold water, bring to a boil, drain, return the beans to the pot and cover with fresh cold water, bring to the boil again, drain the beans one more time and return to the pot. Cover with 10 cups (2.2 L) of water, bring to a boil, then reduce to a simmer, and continue to cook until the beans are tender, approximately 30 minutes. Set aside in the cooking water.

In a large pot, heat the oil, add the onion and garlic. Cook until softened, then add the carrot, zucchini and celery. Sauté uncovered until soft, add the sui choy, tomato paste and spinach. Continue to cook covered until the vegetables are al dente.

Strain the beans, saving the liquid. Put the bean liquid into the vegetable pot. Divide the beans in half, place half in the Cuisinart and purée. Toss the remaining half in the pot with the vegetables. Add the puréed beans to the pot along with the stock, basil, sea salt and pepper to taste. Add the bread and cook for 10 more minutes.

Garnish with the crispy pancetta, Parmesan, parsley and a good drizzle of estate olive oil, like Tenuta del Numerouno.

CAREN'S ADVICE

Estate olive oil is one of those very special oils where the fruit is not only grown on one single estate but pressed and bottled on the premises. It is usually an unfiltered oil which gives it a cloudy look. When you come across it, buy it and treasure the flavor as it is indeed unique. If such a gem is not available where you live, use the best oil you have.

Roasted Corn Chowder

Without a doubt, it is the unique flavor of La Chinata smoked Spanish paprika that turns this chowder into a soup you won't soon forget.

4	cobs of fresh corn	4
4 oz	pancetta, chopped	100 g
1/3 cup	extra virgin olive oil	80 mL
1	large yellow onion, diced	1
1	large leek, white part only	1
2	cloves garlic, minced	2
3	celery stalks, diced	3
2 tsp	smoked paprika, *LA CHINATA*	10 mL
1/2 cup	chopped parsley	120 mL
6 cups	chicken or vegetable stock, *MAJOR*	1.4 L
1	large potato, peeled and diced	1
1 cup	half and half, or whole milk	240 mL
2–5	dashes Worcestershire sauce	2–5
to taste	piri piri or hot sauce (see p. 54)	
to taste	sea salt	
to taste	freshly ground tellicherry or black pepper	

SERVES 6–8

CHIPOTLE CREAM

1 cup	sour cream or crème fraîche	240 mL
1–2	chipotle chilies, minced	1–2

MAKES 1 CUP (240 ML)

Remove all the silk from the corn. Cut the kernels off with a serrated knife. Place the kernels in a hot cast iron frying pan with the pancetta. Fry until the corn is slightly blackened and the pancetta is crisp. Remove and set aside.

In the same pan, add the olive oil, onion, leek, garlic and celery. Fry until the vegetables begin to brown. Stir in the paprika. Add the parsley, stock, potato and reserved corn and pancetta. Simmer for about 20 minutes.

Pour in the cream or milk, Worcestershire sauce, hot sauce, sea salt and pepper to taste. Heat through, taking extreme caution not to let it boil or the cream will curdle.

Ladle the soup into bowls and garnish with a dollop of chipotle cream.

CHIPOTLE CREAM
Mix together. Chill until serving.

CAREN'S ADVICE
I like to use a MSG-free bouillion paste called Major.

Vegetarian Black Bean Soup

If all things that are good for you tasted this good…hold me back!

3 cups	black turtle beans	720 mL
1/3 cup	olive oil, *PRIMAVERA*	80 mL
1	large yellow onion	1
4	garlic cloves, minced	4
3	celery stalks, diced	3
to taste	sea salt and cracked pepper	
8 cups	chicken stock, *MAJOR*	1.9 L
2 tsp	ground cumin	10 mL
1 tsp	ground coriander seed	5 mL
1 tsp	Mexican oregano	5 mL
2	bay leaves	2
1	diced jalapeño, or 1 tbsp (15 mL) caribe chile flakes	1
1 bunch	fresh cilantro, chopped	1 bunch

GARNISH

1/2 cup	tequila (optional)	120 mL
	sour cream or Asiago cheese	
	piri piri sauce (optional) (see p. 54)	

SERVES 8–10

Sort the beans, taking care to remove any small black stones. Place the beans in a large pot and cover with cold water. Bring to a boil, then drain. Cover the beans with fresh water and bring to the boil again. Drain again and set aside.

In a large soup pot, heat the oil. Add the onion, garlic and celery. Sauté until the vegetables are limp. Add the salt and pepper, drained black beans, stock, cumin, coriander, oregano, bay leaves, and jalapeño. Let the soup simmer until the beans are soft. Stir in the chopped cilantro.

Adjust the salt and pepper to suit your taste. If you like really thick soup, remove 2 cups (480 mL) of the beans, purée them and stir them back into the soup.

Garnish with a splash of the tequila and a generous dollop of sour cream or grated cheese. Piri piri is a nice hot finish if you like it extra spicy.

CAREN'S ADVICE

If you prefer more substance to your soup and you are not a vegetarian, cube 1/2 lb (225 g) of bacon or pancetta and fry it along with the onion mixture.

Michel Jacob,
Wolfgang Von Wieser,
Jacques Pepin,
Adam Busby,
me and John Bishop

Lobster Bisque

The sheer decadence of this soup generally steers most cooks into making reservations at a restaurant where it appears on the menu. I have worked at this to simplify and foolproof it so even the most timid of cooks can conquer their fear of Lobster Bisque.

3 lb	small fresh lobsters	1.35 kg
1/3 cup	extra virgin olive oil	80 mL
3 tbsp	unsalted butter	45 mL
1	large yellow onion, diced	1
2	carrots, diced	2
2	celery stalks, diced	2
4	whole garlic cloves, unpeeled	4
2 tsp	tarragon	10 mL
2	large sprigs fresh thyme	2
1	bay leaf	1
1/2 cup	brandy [divided into two 1/4 cups (60 mL)]	120 mL
2 cups	white wine	480 mL
4 cups	chicken or fish stock	960 mL
3 cups	Béchamel Sauce (see p. 178)	720 mL
1/4 cup	port wine or sherry	60 mL
1 cup	crushed tomatoes	240 mL
2 tsp	saffron threads, pounded	10 mL
1 1/2 cups	heavy cream	360 mL
	pinch of cayenne	

SERVES 6–8

Split the lobsters in half and clean. Cut the halves into several pieces, crack the claws and legs and set aside. In a large soup pot melt the oil and butter, add the onion, carrots, celery and garlic. Sweat the vegetables until soft, but not browned, about 5–8 minutes. Add the chopped lobster pieces, tarragon, thyme and bay leaf. Sauté until the lobster turns bright red. Pour 1/4 cup (60 mL) of the brandy into the pot and ignite. Then pour in the wine and stock. Cover and simmer for 20 minutes.

Prepare the béchamel sauce, set aside.

Remove the lobster pieces with a slotted spoon and let them cool slightly. Then remove the meat from the shells. Set aside and pour port wine or sherry over top.

Place shells into pot with crushed tomatoes, béchamel and pounded saffron. Let soup simmer 30–40 minutes.

Pour through very fine strainer, pressing hard on shells and vegetables to extract liquid and achieve maximum flavor. Return soup to pot and add cream, cayenne and remaining 1/4 cup (60 mL) brandy. When heated through, add reserved lobster meat and marinating port. Season to taste.

Soba Noodle and Barbecued Duck

Pasta salad becomes far more than noodles and dressing when this combination is used. Soba or buckwheat noodles have a dense, nutty flavor when married with an Asian dressing and barbecued duck. There are many versions—use cooked chicken or turkey, shrimp, scallops or salmon instead of duck, or go vegetarian.

1	barbecued duck (from a good Chinese take-out or deli counter)	1
1 (8 oz)	pkg of soba noodles or cellophane rice noodles	1 (227g)
1 cup	fresh cilantro, chopped	240 mL
2 tbsp	fresh mint, chopped	30 mL

DRESSING

1	shallot, finely minced	1
4 tbsp	soy sauce	60 mL
2 tbsp	rice vinegar	30 mL
1 tbsp	fermented black beans, chopped	15 mL
1 tbsp	fresh ginger, minced	15 mL
2	large garlic cloves, minced	2
1 tbsp	chili paste (optional)	15 mL
2 tbsp	toasted black sesame seeds	30 mL
2 tbsp	toasted white sesame seeds	30 mL
2 tbsp	sesame oil, *KADOYA*	30 mL
3/4 cup	grapeseed oil	180 mL

1	red pepper, julienned	1
1	large carrot, julienned	1
1	zucchini julienned, use only the green part	1

GARNISH

scallion flowers or chive blossoms

SERVES 6–8

Remove the skin and bones from the duck and discard. Shred the meat and set aside. Cook the noodles al dente, rinse in cold water and set aside to drain.

Prepare the dressing by combining the shallot, soy sauce, vinegar, beans, ginger, garlic and chili paste, if using, and sesame seeds. Then slowly pour the oils into the bowl, whisking by hand the entire time. Taste for seasoning.

Pour the dressing over the cooked noodles, add the raw julienned vegetables and reserved duck, toss well to coat. Turn onto a serving platter. Garnish with scallion flowers or chive blossoms in season.

CAREN'S ADVICE: ZUCCHINI GREEN (SKIN)
Cut the zucchini lengthwise into quarters. Remove as much of the pulp as possible by slicing close to the skin. This will give you the vibrant green color without the spongy, soft center. Perfect for garnish or salads.

Caren's Grilled Caesar Salad

And so the story goes: Tijuana, Mexico, the birthplace of the single most popular salad ordered in restaurants. Alex Cardini was the owner of a restaurant located in the Hotel Caesar in Tijuana and is credited with its creation. One day, a group of hungry patrons entered his restaurant towards the end of service. Most of his supplies had been used, with the exception of romaine lettuce, eggs, garlic, lemon, Parmesan cheese, olive oil and a few stale rolls. Alex proceeded to toss what would become the first Caesar Salad. My version supports the classic dressing. However, due to the inconsistent quality of romaine lettuce, I started to grill it lightly prior to serving. It rocks!

2	cloves garlic, chopped	2
1 tsp	Worcestershire sauce	5 mL
1/2	small fresh lemon, juice of	1/2
1 tbsp	Dijon mustard	15 mL
1	egg yolk	1
6	anchovy fillets	6
1 tsp	freshly ground tellicherry or black pepper	5 mL
1/2 cup	extra virgin olive oil	120 mL
1	large head romaine lettuce	1
GARNISH		
1/2 cup	shaved Parmesan cheese	120 mL

SERVES 6

To make the dressing, place the garlic, Worcestershire sauce, lemon juice, mustard, egg yolk, anchovies and pepper in the bowl of a Cuisinart fitted with a metal blade. Pulse a few times, stopping to scrape down the sides of the bowl.

With the machine running, slowly pour in the olive oil in a thin, steady stream, until the dressing emulsifies and becomes smooth and creamy. Taste, adjust the seasonings and chill until ready to serve.

Remove the outer leaves from the romaine and discard. Cut in sixths taking care to leave the core intact. This will prevent the lettuce from falling apart. Heat your barbecue grill or cast iron fry pan to high. Lightly brush the inside and outside of the lettuce with olive oil and place it cut side down on the hot surface for about 2 minutes. Turn once.

To serve, transfer the lettuce to your serving plate, spoon the dressing over top and garnish with the Parmesan cheese shavings.

Nut-Crusted Chèvre Salad

Woolwich Dairy is the award-winning producer of this fabulous goat cheese available across Canada. It is creamy and smooth with a terrific flavor. I have nut crusted it and dressed it with a walnut oil and sherry vinaigrette to make a great-tasting dinner salad. Let's hear it for Canadian chèvre.

1 1/2 lbs	chèvre, *WOOLWICH DAIRY*	500 g
3/4 cup	toasted ground walnuts	180 mL
6	thin slices french bread	6

DRESSING
1	large shallot minced	1
2 tbsp	Dijon mustard	30 mL
3 tbsp	20-year-old sherry vinegar	45 mL
2/3 cup	walnut oil, *LAPALISSE*	150 mL
to taste	sea salt	
to taste	freshly ground pepper	

3 cups	mixed greens of your choice	720 mL

GARNISH

more toasted ground walnuts (optional)

SERVES 8

Divide the cheese into 8 equal portions, roll in the toasted nuts and place the rounds onto the bread slices. Transfer to a cookie sheet and set aside.

DRESSING
Mix all the ingredients for the dressing together except for the walnut oil. Slowly whisk in the oil and adjust the seasoning with sea salt and pepper. Set aside.

Preheat the broiler, set the cheese disks under the broiler and toast until golden. Toss the greens with the dressing, place the greens on your serving plate and top with the warm chevre cheese. Serve warm, garnish with additional walnuts if desired.

CAREN'S ADVICE
Huileries de Lapalisse makes one of the best nut oils in France. Cold pressed, full of rich nutty intensity, it is a quality worth looking for.

Celery Root Salad

"Celeriac," in its fresh state, closely resembles horseradish root. Its skin is rather knobby and pale, with a crunchy yet mild celery flavor, making it perfect for salads. However, in Canada, the fresh version is not commonly available. Out of all the canned veggies globally available, it is my opinion that only about 5 are really worth the purchase. Celery root is one of them. You can purchase it julienned and ready to go. Its crisp, alive flavor makes this recipe one worth trying!

Rinse the celery root well with cold water. Drain and blot with cloth kitchen towels. Chill until prep time.

DRESSING

In a large bowl, mix together the minced garlic and Dijon mustard and vinegar, then slowly pour in the walnut oil, whisking while pouring. The dressing should be smooth and thick. Add the sea salt and pepper to taste, set aside.

Place the celery root, sweet onion, red peppers, olives, asparagus and carrot in a large serving bowl. Toss to mix. Pour the dressing over and ensure that the salad is coated evenly. Garnish with edible flowers or a mixture of chopped mixed fresh herbs.

4 cups	jarred celery root, rinsed and drained	950 mL
1/2 cup	sweet onion, sliced thin	120 mL
2 cups	roasted red peppers, diced (jarred are fine)	480 mL
1 cup	kalamata olives	240 mL
1 lb	fresh asparagus spears, cooked and chopped	455 g
1 cup	carrot, julienned	240 mL

DRESSING

2	garlic cloves, minced	2
2 tbsp	Dijon mustard	30 mL
1/4 cup	tarragon or white wine vinegar, *DELOUIS*	60 mL
3/4 cup	walnut oil, *LAPALISSE*	180 mL
to taste	sea salt	
to taste	freshly ground tellicherry or black pepper	

GARNISH

chopped mixed herbs
or edible flowers

SERVES 8–10

CAREN'S ADVICE:

Celery root is a gnarly looking root vegetable in its fresh state. Once peeled and shredded, it makes for a great salad. Hugely popular in France, this vegetable debuts primarily jarred in North America. Once drained and chilled, it is delicious any way you choose to prepare it.

Stacked and Layered Salad

Food is fashion and so is its presentation. Height has become an art form in presenting salads and desserts. The wow factor is easily obtained, eclipsing the former flat, spread-out versions of years past. The easiest way to achieve the stacked or layered look is with rings, but you can also use other shapes. Choose one you like and start building your creation.

1 1/2 cups	Crème Fraîche (see p. 180) or sour cream	360 mL
3 tbsp	creamy horseradish	45 mL
	fresh ground tellicherry or black pepper	
1	recipe Avocado Papaya Salsa (see p. 179)	1
4 cups	mixed baby salad greens	950 mL
1 lb	fresh crab or shrimp, cooked, or smoked salmon	455 g
3	yellow or red tomatoes, sliced	3

GARNISH

Balsamic Syrup (see p. 176)

SERVES 6

Mix the Crème Fraîche or sour cream, horseradish and pepper together and set aside.

Place a 2-inch (5-cm) metal ring on your serving plate, drop a generous spoonful of guacamole inside it and spread to meet the edges of the ring. Drop in a handful of salad greens, drizzle a little horseradish cream over top, then your crab, shrimp or smoked salmon and tomato slices. Repeat, making 2 complete layers per serving. Press down lightly so the layers adhere.

Repeat, dividing the ingredients evenly among six servings. Garnish with small drizzles of Balsamic Syrup.

Hoshino Sun, me, Executive chef for Japan Airlines and sôus-chef

Grilled Portobello and Spinach Salad

Spinach salad is just that, spinach salad. It turns into a "wow" factor when you add the special bacon garnish. The author Sharon Tyler Herbst, a friend of mine, was once my guest when I hosted the Food and Wine Show on CKNW/98. During our interview she spoke of this bacon garnish in her then-new book *Never Eat More Than You Can Lift* (Broadway Books). I went home, tried it, and was forever addicted. Make your spinach salad one of divine pleasure. It's all in the garnish!

2 tbsp	extra virgin olive oil, *McEVOY* to sauté the mushrooms	30 mL
1–2	garlic cloves	1–2
2	shallots, minced	2
2	fresh portobello mushrooms, sliced lengthwise	2
to taste	sea salt	
to taste	ground tellicherry or black pepper	
3 tbsp	mango vinaigrette (store bought)	45 mL
6 tbsp	extra virgin olive oil, *McEVOY*	90 mL
2	bunches fresh young spinach, stemmed, washed and dried	2
¹/₂ cup	soft goat cheese	120 mL

SHARON'S GARNISH

1 lb	lean bacon, diced	455 g
3 tbsp	sugar	45 mL
¹/₂ tsp	allspice, ground	2.5 mL
1 tsp	cracked black pepper	5 mL
2 tbsp	water	30 mL

SERVES 6

Heat 2 tbsp (30 mL) of oil in a fry pan. Add the garlic and shallots, soften for about 1 minute. Add the Portobello slices and sauté on both sides until soft, season with sea salt and pepper, set aside—they can be served warm or cold.

Whisk together the mango vinaigrette with the 6 tbsp (90 mL) olive oil, drizzle over the spinach greens and toss well to coat the leaves. Add a touch of salt and pepper. To serve, divide the greens between your serving plates, top with 2 slices of mushroom, a crumbling of cheese and finally the bacon garnish.

GARNISH

To make the garnish, fry the bacon very crisp and drain well on paper towels. Wipe the pan clean, return the crisp bacon to the pan. Mix the sugar, allspice, pepper and water together. Pour over the cooked bacon, tossing to coat. Cook for about 3 minutes. Turn out onto a parchment-lined tray, separating the pieces. Let dry. Sprinkle on top of the salad.

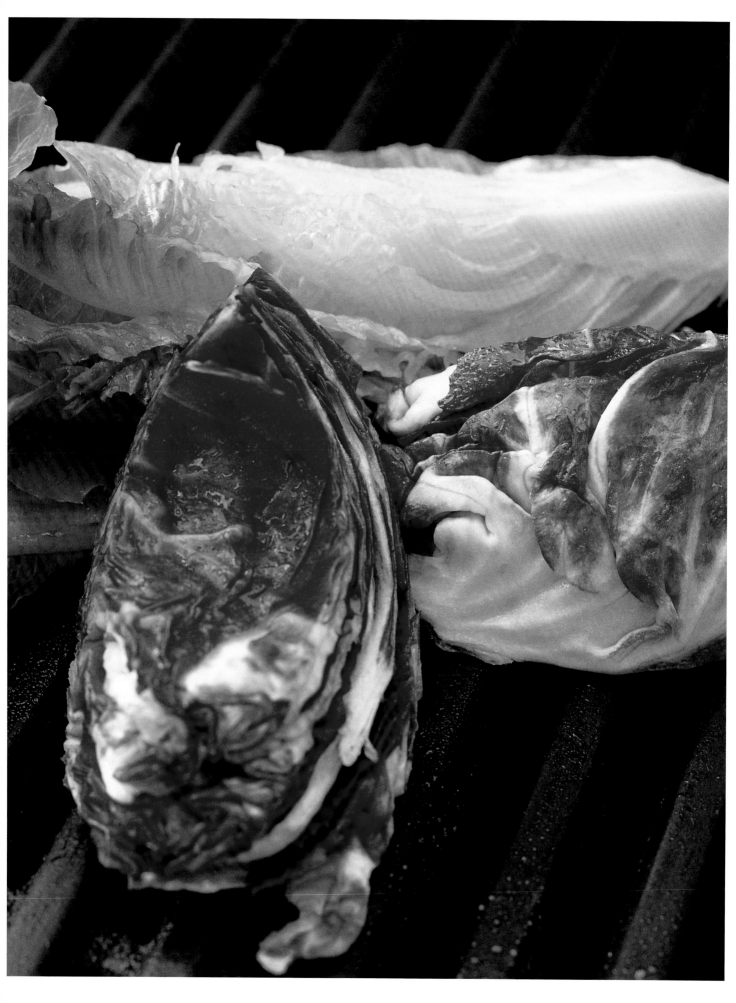

Grilled Romaine and Radicchio Salad

Radicchio—that lovely red Italian lettuce you either love or hate. It has a pronounced bitterness that works well with dressings that are on the sweet side or, as I do it here, brushed with oil and grilled. It takes to the barbecue well because of its strong leaves.

FETA AND FRESH DILL DRESSING

1	small egg	1
4 oz	feta cheese, crumbled	114 mL
1–2	large cloves of garlic, chopped	1–2
1 cup	extra virgin olive oil	240 mL
2 tbsp	fresh lemon juice, approx.	30 mL
2 tbsp	fresh chives, snipped	30 mL
2 tbsp	fresh dill, chopped	30 mL
to taste	sea salt	
to taste	freshly ground black pepper	
1	head Italian radicchio, cut into eighths, do not core	1
1	head young, firm romaine lettuce, cut into eighths, do not core	1
	olive oil for brushing	

GARNISH

1/2 cup	pine nuts, toasted	120 mL

SERVES 6

DRESSING

Place the egg, feta and chopped garlic in a blender or Cuisinart. Run until the garlic is puréed and the cheese is smooth. Slowly pour the olive oil through the feed tube while the motor is running. The dressing should be thick and smooth.

Add the lemon juice—the amount will depend on how tart you like your dressing. Start with 1 tbsp (15 mL) and increase it to suit your tastes. Stir in the chives and dill. Add the sea salt and pepper to taste. Chill until ready to serve.

Heat a cast iron griddle or barbecue. Lightly brush both sides of the lettuces with oil, lay on the hot griddle for about 2–3 minutes or until the lettuce begins to wilt. Turn over and repeat on the other side.

Place on a salad plate, spoon some of the dressing over and garnish with the toasted pine nuts.

CAREN'S ADVICE: TOASTING PINE NUTS

Preheat your oven to 300°F (165°C). Place the pine nuts on a baking sheet and toast for about 15 minutes or until golden brown. Shake the pan during cooking to promote even browning.

Fresh Artichoke and Sweet Pea Salad

It's an unusual combo of veggies, but does this taste ever rock. I always use the smallest baby peas available and, when combined with the crispy shallots, it's a taste you won't forget easily. If you can find fresh baby artichokes, use them. They have no choke so simply peel and boil. It's that easy.

15	fresh baby artichokes or	15
2 (14 oz)	cans of artichokes, drained	2 (398 mL)
2 tbsp	white vinegar	30 mL
6	large shallots, sliced	6
2 tbsp	extra virgin olive oil	30 mL
2 lb	bag of frozen sweet peas	900 g
2 tbsp	balsamic vinegar, *DEL DUCA*	30 mL
1/3 cup	extra virgin olive oil	75 mL
to taste	sea salt	
to taste	ground tellicherry or black pepper	

GARNISH

1 cup	Romano or Parmesan cheese, shaved	240 mL

SERVES 6–8

If you are using fresh artichokes, peel them and trim the bottom being careful not to remove too much. Place them in a large pot of boiling water, add the white vinegar and boil for about 8 minutes. Drain and refresh in cold water. The vinegar prevents the artichokes from turning brown.

While the artichokes are boiling, fry the shallots crispy in the olive oil. Thinly slice the artichokes lengthwise and add them to the shallots. Keeping the heat on low, stir until the ingredients are combined.

Bring a large pot of salted water to the boil. Add the peas and cook for about 3 minutes. Refresh in cold water and drain. Turn the peas onto a serving platter or bowl. Add the shallots and artichokes. Deglaze the pan with the balsamic vinegar, pour in the 1/4 cup (60 mL) of olive oil and add the sea salt and pepper.

Pour the dressed artichokes and shallots over the peas and toss to coat. The dressing can be made in advance to this point and refrigerated. Adjust the seasoning with sea salt and pepper, garnish with the cheese shavings and serve.

Gramma Clara's

Old-Fashioned Potato Salad

Potatoes … mashed, fried, baked, boiled, roasted and, more often than not, salad. The potato is one of the first vegetables to be used as a salad. There are many versions around, but my Mom's is still a personal favorite, perhaps because it appeares at all our family picnics and barbecues. You'll love it too.

4	large Idaho potatoes, boiled with the skin on	4
12	large eggs, hard boiled for 10 minutes	12
4	green onions, finely chopped	4
1/4 cup	fresh parsley, finely chopped	60 mL
3/4 cup	mayonnaise, *HELLMAN'S*	180 mL
1 tsp	Dijon mustard	5 mL
1/2 tsp	hot dog mustard, *FRENCH'S*	2.5 mL
to taste	sea salt	
to taste	freshly ground tellicherry or black pepper	

SERVES 6

Remove the skin from the potatoes and using a wire egg slicer, cut in both directions to make a small dice. Peel the eggs and slice in the same manner. Place the eggs and potatoes in a bowl, add the chopped green onions, parsley, mayonnaise and both mustards. Mix to combine. Take care not to over mix or the salad will become mushy. Season with sea salt and ground pepper. Chill until serving.

Clara McSherry doing what she does best!

Middle Eastern Couscous Salad

Middle Eastern couscous is not the common small-grained couscous with which most of us are familiar. This is a larger toasted variety that swells to the size of tiny peas. The texture is far more interesting than regular couscous. Leftover salad is particularly good for lunch the next day.

1/2 cup	sweet port or Madeira	120 mL
1 cup	Black Mission figs, cut into quarters	240 mL
3 tbsp	unsalted butter	45 mL
1	large Spanish onion, sliced	1
2	cloves garlic, minced	2
1/2	jalapeño pepper, finely diced (optional)	1/2
1 tsp	ground cinnamon	5 mL
1 tsp	saffron threads, pounded into a powder	5 mL
1 1/2 tsp	ground cumin	7.5 mL
1 tsp	ground cardamom	5 mL
5 cups	chicken stock	1.2 L
3 cups	toasted Middle Eastern couscous	720 mL
2	large red bell peppers, roasted and diced or 14 oz (420 mL) can or jar	2
1/2 cup	fresh parsley, chopped	120 mL
1/2 cup	fresh cilantro, chopped	120 mL
1/4 cup	fresh mint, chopped	60 mL
to taste	sea salt	
to taste	freshly ground black pepper	

GARNISH

1 cup	natural pistachio nuts, toasted and chopped	240 mL

SERVES 6–8

Heat the port or Madeira in a small pot, add the figs and simmer for about 5 minutes, or until most of the port is absorbed. Set aside.

Melt the butter in a large frying pan, and add the onion, garlic and jalapeño if using. Sauté until the onion is golden brown. Add the cinnamon, cumin and cardamom, and continue to cook for another minute.

Bring the chicken stock to a boil, add the couscous and saffron, let it simmer for about 5 minutes, or until all of the stock is absorbed. Stir in the onion spice mixture, diced peppers, marinated figs and port. Fold in the fresh herbs and adjust the seasoning with salt and pepper. Turn onto a decorative serving platter and garnish with the toasted pistachios.

Tuna Rolls on Thai Salad

The salad roll takes on a new dimension when the roll is hot and the salad is cold.

1-1$\frac{1}{2}$ lb	fresh tuna	455-675g
2 tbsp	peanut or grapeseed oil	30 mL
3 large	garlic cloves, minced	3
3 tbsp	fresh ginger, minced	45 mL
1 tsp	serano chili, finely minced (optional)	5 mL
1 stalk	fresh lemon grass, minced, tender part only	1
to taste	sea salt	
to taste	freshly ground tellicherry or black pepper	
	rice paper wrappers	

SALAD

1 (7 oz)	pkg cellophane noodles	1 (200g)
$\frac{1}{4}$	head sui choy/Napa cabbage, shredded	$\frac{1}{4}$
2	large carrots, shredded	2
1	red pepper, finely julienned	1
10	dry Chinese mushrooms, soaked in warm water, squeezed dry and julienned	10
$\frac{1}{3}$ cup	fresh basil, shredded	80 mL
$\frac{1}{4}$ cup	fresh mint, shredded	60 mL
1	English cucumber, cut into $\frac{1}{8}$-inch (.2-cm) matchstick strips	1

DRESSING

1 tbsp	sesame oil	15 mL
2 tbsp	fish sauce	30 mL
1 tbsp	rice vinegar	15 mL
3 tbsp	soy sauce	45 mL
1	garlic clove, minced	1
2 tsp	ginger, minced	5 mL
1 tbsp	wasabi paste	15 mL
$\frac{1}{2}$ cup	peanut or grapeseed oil	120 mL

GARNISH

black sesame seeds

SERVES 6–8

Slice the tuna into three 1-inch (2.5-cm) pieces, set aside. Mix the oil, garlic, ginger, chili (if using), lemon grass, sea salt and pepper together. Rub this paste onto the tuna pieces, set aside. Soak the rice paper wrappers in warm water and blot dry on cloth kitchen towels. Lay the damp papers on your work surface. Place one piece of seasoned tuna on one end of a piece of rice paper and roll up, enclosing the tuna completely. Repeat until all the tuna pieces are wrapped. Cover with a damp cloth until ready to cook.

SALAD

Cook and drain the noodles, cutting them with scissors to make them easier to toss. Combine all the salad ingredients in a large bowl. Set aside in refrigerator.

DRESSING

Whisk all the ingredients together except for the peanut or grapeseed oil. Slowly pour in the peanut or grapeseed oil, whisking as you pour. Adjust the seasonings to suit your taste. Set aside.

TO SERVE

Heat a nonstick pan to medium heat. Fry the tuna rolls on all sides until browned and crispy. Keep warm. Pour the dressing over the salad ingredients and toss to combine. Ensure that the vegetables are coated evenly. Place a portion of the dressed salad on your serving plate, top with the crisp tuna roll and garnish with black sesame seeds.

Eggplant Rolls

The directions for this may sound a little tedious, but once the eggplant is grilled the rest is easy. Zucchini could replace eggplant if you prefer.

3	Japanese eggplants	3
	olive oil for grilling	
	sea salt for seasoning	
	freshly ground pepper	
1 (14oz)	jar or can roasted red peppers	1 (400 g)
4 tbsp	balsamic vinegar, infused or plain	60 mL
2	heads roasted garlic, separated, peeled and kept whole (see p. 174)	2
1 (8oz)	jar mini artichokes, *PIACERI DALL ORTO*, cut in half	1 (240 g)
12–15	rosemary branches or bamboo skewers	12–15

MAKES 12–15

Slice the eggplant lengthwise as thinly as possible. Heat a grill to high, brush the eggplant with olive oil, season with salt and pepper and grill for about 2 minutes each side or until the eggplant is cooked but not overdone. Remove and lay on your work surface. Lightly brush each strip with the balsamic vinegar.

Drain the red pepper and blot dry on paper towels. Cut to the same width as the eggplant. Brush an eggplant slice with balsamic vinegar. Lay a red pepper slice on top. Take $1/2$ an artichoke and place it on the end of the roll. Roll the strip up, enclosing the artichoke in the middle. Pierce the roll through the center with the rosemary branch or bamboo skewer. Just as the skewer comes out the other side, pierce with a garlic clove to complete.

Place on a colorful serving platter. Serve at room temperature.

Potato Galette

This is a fabulous way to serve potatoes. The only catch is you need a good nonstick pan to make it easy. If Swiss cheese is not available you can substitute grated Parmesan, Monterey Jack or even a gorgonzola. Whichever way you slice this, it will be wonderful.

	olive oil for brushing the pan	
3	large russet potatoes, peeled and thinly sliced	3
1 cup	Swiss Gruyère cheese, shredded	240 mL
to taste	freshly ground tellicherry or black pepper	
to taste	fleur de sel	

SERVES 4–6

Heat an 8-inch (20-cm) nonstick frying pan to medium and brush with a little olive oil. Lay the potatoes in the pan, overlapping each slice just a little, creating an even layer of potato.

Sprinkle the grated cheese over top of the potato slices, then lay another layer of potato slices over the cheese.

Increase the heat to a medium high and fry the potato cake for about 4 minutes. Flip it over to cook the other side, about another 3 minutes, or until golden brown.

Cut the potato into wedges, finish with a grinding of fresh pepper and a sprinkle of fleur de sel.

CAREN'S ADVICE
To slice the potatoes thinly, use a plastic Japanese slicer, available in good kitchen shops. A very sharp knife would also work well.

Mediterranean New Potato Salad

This is unlike any potato salad you have ever had, in so far as the potatoes are pan fried first to give them a golden brown outer crust. The dressing is then poured over the warm potatoes. This method allows the warm potato to act as a sponge absorbing the dressing. The lemon olive oil is the burst of flavor that gives this dressing its Mediterranean flair. If "O" lemon olive oil is unavailable, substitute with regular extra virgin olive oil and 1 tsp (5 mL) of lemon zest.

$^1/_3$ cup	extra virgin olive oil	80 mL
3	garlic cloves, minced	3
2 lb	small new potatoes, red or white, cut into 1$^1/_2$-inch (3.8-cm) pieces	900 g
1 (14oz)	jar artichokes, *PIACERI DALL ORTO,* drained and quartered	1 (398 mL)
1 (14oz)	can hearts of palm, sliced into $^1/_2$-inch (1.2-cm) pieces	1 (398 mL)
1 cup	kalamata or green olives	240 mL

DRESSING

$^2/_3$ cup	"O" lemon olive oil	150 mL
3 tbsp	sherry wine vinegar	45 mL
2 tbsp	fresh dill, chopped	30 mL
to taste	sea salt	
to taste	freshly ground tellicherry or black pepper	

GARNISH

6 oz	feta cheese	170 mL

SERVES 8

Heat the oil and garlic in a large pan, add the potatoes and cook until lightly browned and tender. Add the artichokes to the pan and toss. Stir in the hearts of palm and olives, tossing to combine. Turn out onto a serving platter.

Mix together the "O" lemon olive oil, vinegar, dill, sea salt and pepper. Pour over the potato mixture and serve at room temperature. Garnish with a crumble of feta.

Asparagus in a Glass

This unique presentation of asparagus can double as a great way to serve a first course at a sit-down dinner or accent a buffet line. I use inexpensive martini glasses and let the asparagus sit in the dressing so there is no passing around of the sauce.

1 1/2 lb	fresh asparagus	680 g

DRESSING

1	garlic clove, minced	1
1 tbsp	strong Dijon mustard	15 mL
2 tbsp	soy sauce	30 mL
2 tbsp	rice vinegar	30 mL
1 tbsp	sesame oil, KADOYA	15 mL
3/4 cup	peanut or grapeseed oil	180 mL
to taste	freshly ground black pepper	

GARNISH

2 tbsp	white sesame seeds, toasted	30 mL
2 tbsp	black sesame seeds, toasted	30 mL

SERVES 6–8

Snap the tough ends from the base of each asparagus stalk and blanch for about 2–3 minutes in a pan of rapidly boiling water. Plunge into cold water to stop the cooking and preserve the color. Wrap in a tea towel and chill until serving.

To make the dressing, mix together the garlic, mustard, soy sauce, vinegar and sesame oil. In a thin steady stream, pour in the peanut or grapeseed oil, whisking while pouring. Add the pepper and adjust the seasoning to suit your tastes.

Pour about 3 tbsp (45 mL)of the dressing in each of the 6–8 martini glasses or other glass containers. Place the asparagus end side down into the dressing, making sure that the containers are full of asparagus. Sprinkle with the sesame seeds. Serve cold.

CAREN'S ADVICE

To roast the sesame seeds, place them in a small baking tray and roast in a 300°F (165°C) oven for about 10 minutes.

Lettuce Wraps

Lettuce wraps are just that: leaves of lettuce used as a wrapper around a filling. It's the Chinese version of a fajita. It makes for a great light appetizer or first course. The filling can be anything you like—shrimp, chicken or even veggies.

1	head iceberg lettuce	1
1	large chicken breast, skinned, boned, diced into ¹/₂-inch (1.2-cm) pieces	1
2 tsp	cornstarch	10 mL
4 tsp	vegetable or corn oil	20 mL
¹/₂ cup	onion, diced	120 mL
¹/₂ cup	Chinese mushrooms, or shiitake, soaked, chopped	120 mL
¹/₂ cup	water chestnuts, chopped	120 mL
4 tbsp	dark soy sauce	60 mL
1 tbsp	fresh ginger	15 mL
1 tsp	chili sauce	5 mL
2 tbsp	sesame oil	30 mL
¹/₄ cup	carrots, diced	60 mL
¹/₄ cup	celery, diced	60 mL
³/₄ tsp	sugar	4 mL
¹/₂ tsp	sea salt	2.5 mL
8 oz	Chinese hoisin sauce	230 g

SERVES 4

Ahead of time, separate the lettuce leaves, rinse under cold water and pat dry with kitchen towels.

In a medium bowl, combine diced chicken breast with cornstarch and rest for 5–10 minutes. Heat oil in a wok over high heat and stir-fry chicken and onion about 1 minute. Add mushrooms, water chestnuts, soy sauce, ginger, chili sauce and sesame oil. Add the carrots and celery with the sugar and salt and stir-fry 1 minute.

Immediately transfer the entire contents of the wok to a heated platter. Spread 2–3 tbsp (30–45 mL) of the mixture onto a lettuce leaf. Drizzle a teaspoon or more to taste of the hoisin on top. Roll up the leaf like a package and enjoy.

CAREN'S ADVICE

Chinese mushrooms are inexpensive and purchased dried. They need to be soaked prior to using. Pour hot water over the mushrooms and let them sit for at least 15 minutes. Drain and squeeze out the excess water. Remove and discard the stem. Julienne or quarter the mushrooms.

José Valagao, and Julia Child

Grilled Mixed Vegetables
with Infused Fruit Balsamic Vinegar

It seems that once we are on to a good thing, it just keeps getting better. Balsamic rapidly paraded its way to first place on the vinegar list with most chefs and cooks. As my good friend Emeril would say, "Kick it up a notch!" Well, that's what the infusion did. Quality balsamic infused with fruit pulp produces a sweet yet tangy version of the classic. I use it when grilling my vegetables for a sensational flavor. Try it—you'll love it!

1	bulb fresh fennel	1
1	sweet onion	1
18	spears of fresh asparagus, preferably on the thick side	18
18	mushrooms	18
1	small zucchini	1
	any other vegetables of choice, such as artichokes, Japanese eggplant, red pepper	
	extra virgin olive oil for basting	
1/2 cup	fruit-infused balsamic vinegar	240 mL
to taste	fleur de sel	
to taste	freshly ground tellicherry or black pepper	

SERVES 6–8

Heat a grill or barbecue to medium-high heat. Cut the vegetables into quarters, ensuring that any cores are kept intact. The cores will hold the vegetables together. Brush the hot grill with oil. Brush the vegetables with vinegar and place on the grill. Let the vegetables cook for about 3–4 minutes each side, depending on their size and thickness.

Continue to brush with the vinegar—the natural sugars will caramelize on the vegetables and give them a fabulous taste. Remove from the grill, drizzle with a little extra virgin oil and season with fleur de sel and ground pepper. Serve hot or at room temperature.

José Valagao,
Emeril Lagasse and me

Grilled Porcini Mushrooms
on Braised Navy Beans

If ever the saying "More beans, please" was applicable, this is it. This first course or lunch is an awesome vegetarian option. The flavors are so well married that, vegetarian or not, you will make it again and again!

2	shallots, finely minced	2
2	garlic cloves, minced	2
3 tbsp	extra virgin olive oil	45 mL
3	large fresh porcini mushrooms	3
1/4 cup	port or sherry	60 mL
to taste	sea salt	
to taste	fresh ground pepper, preferably tellicherry	

BRAISED BEANS

3 tbsp	olive oil	45 mL
2	large yellow onions, diced	2
1/3 cup	port wine or sweet sherry	80 mL
3 tbsp	balsamic vinegar, DEL DUCA	45 mL
2/3 cup	sun-dried tomatoes, chopped	160 mL
6	ripe Roma tomatoes, chopped	6
1/2 lb	Blue Moon, Gorgonzola or Cambozola cheese, cut into cubes	225 g
2	heads roasted garlic, cooled, peeled and left whole (see p. 174)	2
to taste	sea salt	
to taste	freshly ground tellicherry or black pepper	
2 cups	fresh arugula, stemmed and washed	240 mL

GARNISH

1/2 cup	basil, finely minced	120 mL

SERVES 6

Sauté the shallots and garlic in the olive oil. Add the mushrooms, cap side down, pour in the port, put the lid on the pan and sauté until the mushrooms are cooked, about 3–5 minutes. They should be firm but soft to the touch.

Season with a sprinkle of sea salt and ground pepper. Set aside.

BRAISED BEANS

Heat the olive oil in a large fry pan, add the diced onions and fry them until they are golden and caramelized. Add the port or sherry and balsamic vinegar, stirring to combine. Stir in the sun-dried tomatoes, Roma tomatoes, cheese and roasted garlic and season with sea salt and pepper.

To assemble the salad, place a handful of the arugula in the center of a plate, place a portion of the bean mixture on top of the greens, then finish with a fan of sliced mushrooms, using 1/2 mushroom per serving. Sprinkle with the basil to finish.

Serve warm or at room temperature.

Grilled Fresh Artichokes with Garlic Aïoli

Artichokes any way are the absolute favorite food of my daughter Christina. Because of their rather unapproachable appearance, most home cooks pass them by. My easy preparation removes the fear and provides you with a gorgeous grilled, tasty first course that you and your guests will savor until the last leaf.

2 tbsp	white vinegar or lemon juice	30 mL
6	large fresh whole artichokes with some stem attached	6
3–4 tbsp	olive oil	45–60 mL
	sea salt	
	freshly ground tellicherry or black pepper	

SERVES 6

GARLIC AÏOLI

3	garlic cloves, peeled	3
2 tbsp	fresh lemon juice	30 mL
1 tbsp	Dijon mustard	15 mL
1	egg yolk	1
2/3 cup	extra virgin olive oil	160 mL
to taste	sea salt	
to taste	freshly ground black pepper	

MAKES 3/4 CUP (180 ML)

Bring a large pot of water to the boil, add the white vinegar or lemon juice to the pot. Drop in the artichokes and boil for about 30–40 minutes, or until tender. Check to see that they are cooked by pulling on 1 or 2 of the leaves—if they pull out easily the artichokes are cooked; if you have to tug, let them boil for another 5 minutes.

Remove the artichokes and drain on kitchen towels. When they are cool enough to handle, cut in half lengthwise, through the stem. Carefully remove the fuzzy choke from the center and scrape away the thorny part.

Heat a large cast iron fry pan to medium hot, add the oil, sprinkle the cut side of the artichokes with sea salt and ground pepper. Place them cut side down into the hot pan and grill for about 5–8 minutes or until golden brown. Transfer onto a tray and keep warm in a hot oven until serving time.

Serve with the Garlic Aïoli or any dipping sauce of your choice.

GARLIC AÏOLI
Place the garlic, lemon juice, mustard and egg yolk into the bowl of a Cuisinart. Purée. With the machine running, slowly pour the olive oil through the feed tube until a thick sauce is formed. Season with the sea salt and pepper.

Lobster Brûlée

A savory version of the ever-popular, in-demand burnt sugar custard. I have lightened it up considerably with the introduction of whole milk and half and half instead of heavy cream—this not only eases the guilt, but saves some room for any courses that may follow.

1	whole head roasted garlic (see p. 174)	1
1 cup	half and half	240 mL
1 cup	whole milk	240 mL
1 tsp	saffron threads,	5 mL
1 tsp	sea salt	5 mL
3	large whole eggs	3
2	large yolks	2
to taste	ground white pepper	
2	shallots, finely diced	2
6 oz	fresh lobster meat, chopped	170 mL
½ cup	fresh grated Parmesan cheese	120 mL

SERVES 6–8

Preheat the oven to 350°F (175°C). Heat together the cream and milk in a heavy bottomed pot. Do not boil. Pound the saffron and sea salt together in a mortar and pestle until they become a powder. Add this to the warmed milk. Beat the eggs and yolks together until they are thick and pale colored. Slowly pour the warmed milk mixture into the beaten eggs, and add the pepper to taste. Pour the egg-milk mixture through a mesh sieve, then into individual ramekins or one large gratin dish.

Sauté the shallots until they are soft but not brown, then divide them with the lobster meat and roasted garlic cloves evenly among the dishes. Place the dishes into a sided baking tray and pour in hot water until it reaches halfway up the sides of the ramekins. Bake at 350°F (175°C) for 45–60 minutes. Remove from the water bath, sprinkle with the Parmesan cheese, place under a broiler or use a hand-held butane torch until the topping is golden brown. Serve hot or at room temperature.

CAREN'S ADVICE
Lobster can be replaced by crab, shrimp, scallops or whatever you prefer.

Me and Jacques Pepin

Prawns, Ouzo and Feta

A very easy one-dish dinner or lunch. A crisp salad goes well with this along with a crusty bread to absorb any lingering juices!

4 tbsp	extra virgin olive oil	60 mL
1	large yellow onion, diced	1
2–3	cloves garlic, minced	2–3
2 cups	tomatoes, diced or crushed	480 mL
1/2 cup	ouzo or Pernod	120 mL
1 tsp	Greek oregano	5 mL
2 tbsp	parsley, finely chopped	30 mL
to taste	sea salt	
to taste	freshly ground tellicherry or black pepper	
1 lb	shelled raw prawns, approx. 26/30 (leave tail shell intact) (see p. 118)	455 g
7 oz	crumbled feta cheese	200 g

GARNISH

scallions, sliced

SERVES 6

Heat the oil in a paella pan or a large high-sided sauté pan. Add the onion and sauté for about 3 minutes. Add the garlic and continue to cook for another 4 minutes. Stir in the tomatoes, ouzo or Pernod, oregano, parsley, sea salt and pepper. Cover and simmer for about 15 minutes.

Preheat the oven to 375°F (190°C). Add the prawns to the sauté and cook for about 5 minutes. Evenly distribute the feta over top and bake for about 5–10 minutes, or until the feta is melted.

Garnish with slices of scallion.

Spinach Florentine

This spinach dish can be served as a side dish or as a bed holding anything from grilled shellfish, salmon or even poached eggs. However you decide to present it, the taste is always outstanding.

3	large bunches of fresh spinach cooked and squeezed dry	3
2	large garlic cloves, minced	2
2 tbsp	unsalted butter	30 mL
2 tbsp	unbleached all-purpose flour	30 mL
1 cup	milk	240 mL
1 cup	Swiss Gruyère cheese, grated	240 mL
1 tsp	sea salt	5 mL
	pinch of fresh ground nutmeg	
1/2 tsp	freshly ground tellicherry or black pepper	2.5 mL

MAKES 2 CUPS (480 ML)

Once the spinach is squeezed dry, chop it finely and place it in a large fry pan. Add the garlic and dry fry on medium heat until all the moisture is gone. Set aside.

In a 1 qt (1.14 L) saucepan, melt the butter, add the flour and cook for 3 minutes. Whisk in the milk and continue whisking until the mixture is smooth and thick. Add the cheese and stir until it melts. Add the reserved spinach along with the seasonings and mix well to combine.

Le Crocodile's Alsatian Onion Tart

Michel Jacob, chef/owner of the very prestigious Le Crocodile Restaurant in Vancouver, serves up one of the best Alsatian Onion Tarts I have ever eaten! Michel hails from Alsace in France and his version is authentic and full of flavor. It can double as a light meal when served with a chèvre salad, chilled Hugel and an interesting dinner date.

1.5 lb	onions	700 g
7 oz	butter	200 g
1 tbsp	olive oil	15 mL
2 oz	all-purpose flour	50 g
2 oz	butter	50 g
1 cup	milk	240 mL
1 cup	cream	240 mL
4	eggs, slightly beaten	4
	sea salt	
	freshly ground black pepper	
	nutmeg	
3.5 oz	bacon, blanched and cut into 1-inch (2.5-cm) strips	100 g
	Quick Short Crust Pastry (see p. 196)	

SERVES 6–8

Peel and thinly slice the onions. Cook in butter and oil without browning for 20 minutes. Prepare a béchamel with the flour, butter and milk (see p. 178). Remove the béchamel from the heat and pour over the onions. Add cream, eggs, salt, pepper, nutmeg and bacon strips to the onions.

Press short crust pastry into a buttered pie dish. Pour béchamel mixture into the pie crust. Bake at 375°F (190°C) for approximately 30 minutes.

Michel Jacob, Clara McSherry and Gary Meister

Home Fries

These are truly the tastiest french fries you will ever eat. They come without guilt as they are not deep-fried but instead are oven-fried in a minimal amount of oil. I always plan on at least 1 large potato per person and then throw in 2 more for the potato lovers at the table. I like to serve them with Garlic Aïoli (see p. 96). Brace yourself, these are truly as good as it gets.

6	large russet potatoes, skin on	6
2–3 tbsp	extra virgin olive oil	30–45 mL
to taste	sea salt	
to taste	freshly ground pepper	

SERVES 4

Scrub the potatoes well and cut them into french fry sticks. Do not make them too big as this increases cooking time. A good size is $^1/_4$ inch (.5 cm) by the length of the potato.

Preheat the oven to 450°F (230°C). Place the potato sticks on a cookie sheet, drizzle the oil over and toss with your hands to coat evenly with oil. Sprinkle with sea salt and pepper. Make sure that they are not piled on top of each other while baking—they like to bask in their own space so that they become golden brown on all sides.

Bake for about 30 minutes or until the fries are golden brown. You will have to turn them once during cooking. If you find them sticking a bit, add a little more oil.

pizza, pasta, rice & bread

Jason's Very Plain Cheese Pizza

My son, Jason is a great little guy. At the age of 3, he watched me stuff the Thanksgiving turkey, then proclaimed himself a vegetarian. He is also the fussiest eater I know. We tease him relentlessly about being the only vegetarian who doesn't eat vegetables. Needless to say, meal times are not the highlight of Jason's day, unless I make his favorite pizza—cheese only and no toppings! If you have any picky eaters, try this.

2 tsp	sugar	10 mL
1/2 cup	warm water	120 mL
1 tbsp	dry yeast	15 mL
3 cups	unbleached flour	720 mL
1 tsp	sea salt	5 mL
3 tbsp	extra virgin olive oil	45 mL
3/4 cup	water	180 mL
1/2 cup	plain tomato sauce, *ITALIA IN TAVOLA*	120 mL
2 cups	mozzarella, grated	480 mL

SERVES 4–6 PICKY EATERS

Dissolve the sugar in the 1/2 cup (120 mL) water, sprinkle the yeast over top and let it sit for about 5 minutes, until it begins to bubble. Place the flour and salt in the bowl of a Cuisinart, add the proofed yeast and olive oil. Turn the machine on and run it while pouring the 3/4 cup (180 mL) water through the feed tube. The dough will form a ball on the side of the bowl. Remove the dough and knead it on a lightly floured surface for a few minutes until it is smooth and elastic. Place the dough in a bowl and lightly oil the top. Place the bowl in a draft-free area for about 40 minutes or until it doubles in size.

Preheat the oven to 500°F (260°C). Lightly oil an 11 x 17 inch (26 x 41 cm) cookie sheet. Press the dough evenly into the pan. Brush the tomato sauce evenly over the dough. Sprinkle the cheese over and bake for about 20 minutes or until the dough is crisp.

CAREN'S ADVICE

For the more adventurous, add any combination of artichokes, olives, capers, red pepper, sweet onion, deli meats, chipotle chili, smoked salmon, brie, Gorgonzola, smoked provolone, pears or prosciutto di Parma.

Romy Prasard's Prosciutto Pizza

I had the pleasure of being part of a Chefs' exchange with the Mexican Trade Commission in Mexico City. It was on that trip that I met Romy Prasard and Andrew Court. We cooked Canadian cuisine and enjoyed a city that held such a culinary intrigue for us all, especially when the secrets of mole were told. Pizza isn't Mexican but it is one of Romy's specialities at his restaurant, Cin Cin.

DOUGH

1/2 cup	warm water	120 mL
1 tsp	dry yeast	5 mL
1 tsp	salt	5 mL
2 cups	all-purpose flour	480 mL
3 tbsp	extra virgin olive oil	45 mL

PROSCIUTTO PIZZA

8	garlic cloves, roasted and coarsely chopped (see p. 174)	8
2	asparagus spears, sliced into thin rounds	2
1 tsp	fresh rosemary, chopped	5 mL
1/2 cup	grated mozzarella	120 mL
6	prosciutto de Parma, shaved pieces	6
1 cup	grana padano cheese, shaved	240 mL
	olive oil to drizzle on finished pizza	

SERVES 6

DOUGH

Combine warm water and yeast until the yeast starts to bubble. Sift salt and flour onto work station and make a well into which you pour the oil and water and yeast mixture. Knead together ingredients until dough is smooth and doesn't stick to your hands. Set aside and let rise until doubled in size. Cut dough into two and roll out very thin onto a floured surface to approximately 12–14 inches (30–35 cm). Preheat oven and a pizza stone to 500°F (260°C) and then assemble your pizzas as directed below.

PROSCIUTTO PIZZA

Evenly spread the dough with the coarsely chopped roasted garlic, asparagus, rosemary and mozzarella. Place on the pizza stone and bake in the oven until the edges are golden, and the center and bottom of the pizzas are cooked. When you remove from the oven, place the shaved, uncooked prosciutto then the grana padano on top. Drizzle with extra virgin olive oil and cut each pizza into 4–8 pieces.

Andrew Court, Romy Pragard and me (Mexico City Chef Exchange)

Fifteen-Minute Gorgonzola Pasta

A very quick and easy one-pot sauce that will knock you over. How can anything that takes 15 minutes taste this good?

1 tbsp	unsalted butter	15 mL
1	shallot, minced	1
1 cup	chicken or vegetable stock, *MAJOR*	240 mL
8 oz	Italian Gorgonzola cheese	240 g
1 lb	pasta, *CARA NONNA*, any shape	454 g

GARNISH

1/2 cup	freshly grated Parmesan cheese	120 mL
1/3 cup	toasted pine nuts	80 mL
1/3 cup	parsley, finely chopped	80 mL

SERVES 4–6

Melt the butter in a heavy bottomed saucepan, add the shallot and sauté until soft. Add the chicken stock and increase the heat to a boil. Boil the stock until it is reduced to 1/2 cup (120 mL). Add the Gorgonzola cheese and turn the heat down to a simmer. Whisk until smooth and creamy. Pour over hot pasta, garnish with Parmesan, pine nuts and parsley.

CAREN'S ADVICE

I prefer to use artisan air dried pastas like Cara Nonna. This pasta allows your sauce to really cling, because of the bronzing and air drying.

Herb-Stuffed Wontons
with Beurre Blanc Sauce

In the food world, quick and easy is seldom synonymous with wow, but it is here! Use fresh wonton wrappers (available at most Asian markets) to make these packets that are a great light start to any dinner. Take care to remove the stems from the flowers and herbs and use only petals. The stems will puncture the packets.

1	package fresh wonton wrappers	1
1 cup	mixed fresh herbs (basil, tarragon, oregano, sage etc), stems removed	240 mL
1 cup	edible flower petals	240 mL

SERVES 6

BEURRE BLANC SAUCE

1/2 cup	white wine	120 mL
2	shallots, minced	2
2 tbsp	tarragon vinegar	30 mL
1/2 lb	cold unsalted butter, cut into small pieces	225 g
	squeeze of fresh lemon juice	
to taste	sea salt	
to taste	freshly ground white pepper	

MAKES 1 CUP (240 ML)

GARNISH

1 cup	Parmesan cheese shavings	240 mL
1/2 bunch	minced parsley	1/2 bunch
	extra fresh flower petals	

Lay the wrappers on your work surface, arrange a few herbs and flower petals in the center, leaving a 1/4-inch (.5-cm) border clear. Brush this border with water, top with another wrapper and, using a rolling pin, press gently to seal. Repeat with remaining wrappers. Dust with a little flour after rolling to prevent sticking. When finished separate the layers with plastic wrap until ready to serve. Remove wrap and cook in salted boiling water for about 2–3 minutes, drain and serve with Beurre Blanc Sauce (see below), Parmesan cheese, finely minced parsley and extra fresh flower petals.

BEURRE BLANC SAUCE

In a small stainless steel pot, combine the wine, shallots and vinegar. Bring to a boil and reduce to 3 tbsp (45 mL) over a low heat. Slowly whisk in the butter 1 tbsp (15 mL) at a time until the sauce is smooth and thick. Finish with a squeeze of lemon, sea salt and white pepper to taste.

Diane's Spicy Singapore Noodles

High school was where I met my life-long best friend, Diane Lawrence. We hated math and loved home economics—the cooking side only! Although teaching was never Diane's forte, mastering the art of flavors of the table certainly was. This is just one of many recipes she has created over the years! Diane, my unsung hero!

1 (1lb)	pkg of rice stick dried noodles	1 (450 g)
10	Chinese dried mushrooms	10
3 tbsp	vegetable or peanut oil	45 mL
2	medium yellow onions, sliced	2
1	head sui choy/Napa cabbage, shredded	1
3	large carrots, julienned	3
1-inch	piece ginger, finely chopped	2.5-cm
1 tbsp	caribe chili flakes	15 mL
1–2 tbsp	curry powder	15–30 mL
1/3 cup	soy sauce	80 mL
2 tbsp	fish sauce	30 mL
20	snow peas, blanched and sliced	20
1/2	bunch cilantro, chopped	1/2
to taste	sea salt	
to taste	ground tellicherry or black pepper	
GARNISH		
	green onions, chopped	
1/2 cup	cashews, chopped	120 mL

SERVES 6–8 DINNER DISH
SERVES 12–20 HORS D'OEUVRES

Cook the noodles in rapidly boiling water for about 3 minutes. Rinse in cold water and wrap in cloth kitchen towel to absorb all moisture. Chill until ready to use.

Soak the mushrooms in a bowl of hot water for about 20 minutes, drain and squeeze dry. Remove the stems and discard. Julienne the mushrooms, and set aside.

Heat the oil in a large skillet, add the onions and cook until well browned, tossing the pan to keep the color even. Add the sui choy and carrots to the onions. Cover and cook for about 3 minutes until the sui choy begins to wilt. Add the mushrooms, ginger, chili flakes, curry, soy sauce and fish sauce, and stir to combine.

Add the noodles to the pan and toss carefully to coat them evenly with the vegetables and seasonings. Be patient as this will take a few minutes. Keep the heat on medium, add the snow peas and cilantro. Toss through. Season with salt and pepper.

If serving as dinner, turn the noodles out onto a serving platter and garnish with green onions and chopped nuts. If using as an hors d'oeuvre, place in small Chinese food take-out tubs and attach chopsticks.

CAREN'S ADVICE

For a more substantial main course, try adding 1/2 lb (225 g) of shrimp meat or leftover chicken, beef or fish.

Susan's Wild Mushroom Pasta

Susan Meister, wonderful friend and owner of Fabulous Foods Catering, very frequently prepares this pasta dish for me, not because that is all she makes, but because it is what I request. Although my daughter Christina moans, "Oh, not again," I never tire of the great woodsy, intense flavor of the mushroom sauce. Thanks, Sue.

6 tbsp	extra virgin olive oil	90 mL
1	small onion, finely chopped	1
2	garlic cloves, minced	2
4 cups	fresh shiitake mushrooms, sliced	950 mL
2 cups	fresh chanterelles, sliced	480 mL
1 1/2 cups	whipping cream	360 mL
1 1/2 cup	chicken stock	360 mL
	sea salt	
	freshly ground black pepper	
1–2 tbsp	chili oil	15–30 mL
1 lb	truffle pasta, *CARA NONNA* or wide egg noodles	454 g

GARNISH

1	bunch fresh cilantro, chopped	1

SERVES 6

Heat fry pan over medium heat. Add 4 tbsp (60 mL) of the olive oil. Add the onion and garlic and sauté until onion is soft and golden. Add the remaining 2 tbsp (30 mL) of oil and the mushrooms and cook until soft and browned and moisture has evaporated.

Add the cream and the stock and simmer until sauce has thickened—about 10 minutes. Add salt and pepper and chili oil to taste. While the sauce is simmering, place the pasta in a large saucepan of boiling water and cook until al dente. Drain the pasta and toss with a drizzle of olive oil. Place the pasta in serving bowls and top with mushroom mixture.

Sprinkle with chopped fresh cilantro and fresh ground pepper. Serve with sautéed green beans or roasted asparagus with grilled chicken breast or escalope of veal.

CAREN'S ADVICE

All the tales of cooking perfect pasta can be put to sleep. The only 2 things required are lots of boiling water and salt. No oil, butter or small devices dropped into the pot. Pasta requires freedom of movement, so that it can cook evenly without gumming together. For a 1.1 lb pkg (500 g) of pasta, bring 4 cups (950 mL) of water to a rolling boil. Add 1 tbsp (15 mL) salt just before adding the pasta. Cook for the required time as per instructed on the packet. NEVER rinse, only drain. Rinsing not only removes nutrients from the pasta, it also affects how the sauce will adhere.

Me and Susan Meister

Penne Puttanesca

If any one dish could swirl controversy, perhaps this is the one. Puttanesca, the sauce, refers to women of the evening who, upon returning home in the wee hours, open the refrigerator to a scant nothing, save perhaps a half tin of anchovies, some withered garlic, tired tomatoes and olives. I have elaborated a bit on the sauce, but the story remains the same. Puttana's pasta—hence puttanesca with penne noodles. The flavor is as fiery as their profession!

¹/₂ cup	extra virgin olive oil	120 mL
¹/₂	bunch green onions, chopped	¹/₂
1	small yellow onion, diced	1
3	garlic cloves, minced	3
4	anchovy fillets, chopped	4
3 tbsp	capers	45 mL
1 cup	kalamata olives, pitted and chopped	240 mL
1–2 tbsp	hot chili flakes	15–30 mL
2 cups	crushed tomatoes	480 mL
1 lb	penne noodles, cooked	455 g
¹/₂	bunch basil, chopped	¹/₂
1 tsp	sea salt	5 mL
¹/₂ tsp	freshly ground tellicherry or black pepper	2.5 mL

GARNISH

2 tbsp	minced parsley	30 mL
	freshly grated Parmesan cheese, preferably Reggiano	

SERVES 6

Heat the oil in a large sauté pan. Add the onions and garlic and fry for about 5 minutes until soft. Stir in the anchovies and sauté until they almost dissolve, about 4 minutes. Add the capers, olives, chili flakes and tomatoes. Reduce the heat and simmer for 10–15 minutes or until the tomatoes break and form a nice, thick sauce. Meanwhile, cook the pasta. Stir the basil, sea salt and pepper into the sauce.

To serve, toss the sauce with the pasta. Garnish with minced parsley. Pass the Parmesan at the table.

New Wave Pasta Niçoise

With tuna being the darling of the sea, what could be better than turning France's favorite bistro salad into North America's favorite pasta?

6 tbsp	extra virgin olive oil	90 mL
1 cup	red onion, diced	240 mL
1	garlic clove, minced	1
4-6	anchovy fillets, chopped	4-6
3 tbsp	balsamic vinegar	45 mL
2 cups	red grape tomatoes, halved	480 mL
24–36	kalamata olives, pitted	24–36
1/2 lb	thin green beans, blanched and cut into 3-inch (7.5-cm) pieces	225 g
1.1 lb	pkg spaghetti, penne or lasagnotti, CARA NONNA	500 g
2 lb	fresh Ahi tuna steaks, grilled to desired doneness	900 g

GARNISH

1/4 cup	each parsley and dill, finely chopped	60 mL
3 tbsp	crispy capers	45 mL
	Parmesan cheese	

SERVES 6

Heat the oil in a large sauté pan. Add the onion and sauté for about 5 minutes. Add the garlic and the anchovies and continue to cook on medium heat until the anchovies are dissolved. Add the balsamic vinegar to the pan, along with the tomatoes, olives and beans. Heat through.

Add the cooked pasta and toss the ingredients together. Break the tuna into chunks, not too small. Add to the pasta and carefully mix through. Don't pulverize the tuna. When heated through, transfer to serving bowls and garnish with chopped herbs, crispy capers and Parmesan cheese.

CAREN'S ADVICE

Blot the capers dry on paper towels. Heat 1/2 cup (120 mL) olive oil in a small pot. Drop the capers into the hot oil until they open and crisp, less than one minute. Drain on paper towel.

Clara's Lasagna

My mother Clara has been making this lasagna for as long as I can remember. It appears at every family get-together for at least one meal. From Chicago to Whistler and all points in between, everyone who has had the pleasure agrees—it is well worth the effort!

2 tbsp	olive oil	30 mL
3 tbsp	unsalted butter	45 mL
2 cups	chopped onion	480 mL
4	large garlic cloves, minced	4
1 lb	lean hamburger meat	455 g
1 lb	regular hamburger meat	455 g
1 tbsp	freshly ground black pepper	15 mL
1/3 cup	finely chopped parsley	80 mL
2 pinches	ground cloves	2
1 tbsp	chicken base, *MAJOR* or 1 cube chicken bouillion	15 mL
7 tbsp	dried oregano, crushed in your hand before adding	105 mL
2 (25 oz)	jars tomato sauce, *ITALIA IN TAVOLA*	2 (700g)
1/2 cup	red wine	120 mL
4	bay leaves	4
	sea salt	
28	no-cook lasagna noodles, the flat ones not the rippled edge variety	28
3 lb	grated mozzarella	1.35 kg
2 cups	grated Parmesan (preferably grana padano)	480 mL

SERVES 8–10

Heat the oil and butter in a large sauté pan. Add the onion and garlic and cook until translucent, but not browned. Add the hamburger meat to the pan and cook for about 5 minutes until it begins to brown. Add the pepper, parsley, cloves, chicken base or cube and oregano. Cook through until nice and browned. Add the tomato sauce, red wine and bay leaves to the pan. Simmer for about 45 minutes. Add sea salt to taste.

Preheat the oven to 275°F (135°C). To assemble, ladle about a 1/2 cup (120 mL) of sauce in the bottom of a 9 x 13 x 3 inch (22.5 x 33 x 7.5 cm) roasting pan. Place a single layer of noodles on the bottom, top with sauce, a generous sprinkle of mozzarella cheese, a light sprinkle of Parmesan, then noodles. Repeat to 4 layers, finishing with sauce, mozzarella and then Parmesan. Bake in the oven for 45 minutes and then increase the temperature to 325°F (165°C) for an additional 45 minutes. Let the lasagna rest for 15 minutes before cutting and serving.

CAREN'S ADVICE

When placing the noodles, alternate the direction with each layer. By alternating the noodles, your lasagna will not slip apart when you cut it.

Clara McSherry multi-tasking in the kitchen

Roasted Chicken Lasagna
with Wild Mushrooms

One of my favorite flavors is wild mushrooms. I seem to gravitate toward them and create recipes around them. This one is so simple— a little sauce, some cooked chicken and mushrooms. A spit-roasted supermarket chicken provides an easy way out, or use leftovers from last night. Either way, this is a terrific dish to enjoy at home or to make you the hero of a potluck.

3 oz	dried wild mushrooms, such as cèpes, chanterelles, boletus or porcinis, PLANTIN	50 g
1	whole roasted chicken (about 2¹/₂ lbs/1.1 kg)	1
¹/₃ cup	olive oil	80 mL
1	large yellow onion, diced	1
2 or 3	garlic cloves, minced	2 or 3

BÉCHAMEL SAUCE

3 tbsp	unsalted butter	45 mL
1	large shallot, minced	1
3 tbsp	unbleached all-purpose flour	45 mL
3 cups	milk	480 mL
¹/₂ tsp	sea salt	2.5 mL
2 tsp	ground white pepper	10 mL
	few grindings of nutmeg	
¹/₂ cup	Romano cheese, freshly grated	120 mL
1 lb	spinach lasagna noodles	455 g
¹/₂ cup	Parmesan cheese, freshly grated	120 mL

SERVES 8

Cover the mushrooms with hot water and let them soak for 30 minutes. Drain, squeeze dry, chop and set aside. Meanwhile, remove the chicken meat from the bones. Discard the skin and shred the meat into small bite-sized pieces. Set aside.

Heat the oil in a fry pan over medium heat. Add the onion and garlic and sauté until the onion is soft. Add the reserved mushrooms and the shredded chicken meat, stirring to combine. Set aside.

BÉCHAMEL SAUCE

Melt the butter in a saucepan. Add the shallot and cook over low heat until softened and translucent but not brown. Stir in the flour and cook for about 3 minutes. Whisk in the milk and continue to whisk until the sauce is thick and smooth. Taste and adjust seasonings with salt, pepper and nutmeg. Add the Romano cheese and set aside.

ASSEMBLE

Cook the noodles until al dente. When noodles are done, drain and lay them flat on a cloth kitchen towel to dry. To assemble, preheat the oven to 350°F (175°C). Lightly oil the bottom of a shallow 3 x 9 x 12 inch (7.5 x 22.5 x 30 cm) baking pan. Lay the noodles evenly on the bottom, spread a portion of the chicken mixture on top, then some of the sauce and a sprinkling of Parmesan cheese. Top with a layer of the cooked noodles.

Repeat 2 more times, finishing with the noodles, sauce and a final sprinkling of cheese. Cover with foil and bake for about 20 minutes.

Sausage and Penne Pasta

Pasta is one of the great saviors of our era. It seems to calm the kids, feed the frenzy and excite the adults, depending on how interesting the ingredients are. I always experiment with new variations and I encourage you to do the same.

1	head garlic, roasted (see p. 174)	1
3 tbsp	olive oil	45 mL
8	medium turkey, chicken or Italian sausages	8
2 cups	large white onion, sliced	480 mL
1/4 cup	balsamic vinegar	60 mL
1 cup	fresh shiitake mushrooms, sliced	240 mL
2	garlic cloves, minced	2
1 cup	thick plain Italian tomato sauce, *ITALIA IN TAVOLA*	240 mL
1/2 cup	wine (whatever is on hand)	120 mL
1/2 cup	chicken or beef stock	120 mL
1 tsp	oregano	5 mL
1/3 cup	parsley, chopped	80 mL
1/2 cup	kalamata olives, pitted and coarsely chopped	120 mL
to taste	sea salt	
to taste	freshly ground black pepper	
1 lb	pkg penne pasta, cooked al dente	500 g

GARNISH

Parmesan cheese, freshly grated

SERVES 6

While the garlic is roasting, heat 1 tbsp (15 mL) of the olive oil in a large sauté pan. Slice the sausages into 1/2-inch (1-cm) pieces and fry on both sides until golden brown and almost cooked through. Transfer the sausage to a small bowl and set aside.

Add the remaining 2 tbsp (30 mL) of oil to the same pan along with the sliced onion. Sauté for about 10 minutes or until the onion begins to brown. Add the balsamic vinegar, sliced shiitakes and the garlic. Stir to combine, scraping the pan to get all the brown bits from the bottom. Add the tomato sauce, wine and stock, stirring to combine. The sauce should not be too thick. If it is, add more wine or a little water. Add the reserved cooked sausage and the oregano, parsley and olives. Let the sauce simmer for a further 10 minutes. Adjust the seasoning with sea salt and fresh ground pepper. Peel the cooled garlic and add the whole peeled cloves to the sauce.

Serve over cooked hot penne noodles or pasta of your choice. Garnish with grated Parmesan cheese.

Me and Herre Poron (Plantin) "King of Mushrooms and Truffles"

Doreen's Creamy Risotto
with Garlic and Prawns

I met Doreen more than 13 years ago. She attended one of my classes, then two, then many. I can identify true culinary junkies very quickly and Doreen was one. Her passion and love of good food solidified our friendship and since 1989 our families have bonded. She was an integral part of my first book, the opening of the new school and a real influence on all the classes that we teach. Doreen and her husband Maury have also been a driving force in our annual charity auction for the BC Child Foundation, behind which we put all our culinary influence. Thank you, the Corday family.

3	whole heads garlic, roasted (see p. 174)	3
4	large shallots, sliced and fried crispy	4
8 cups	chicken or fish stock	2 L
2 tbsp	unsalted butter	30 mL
1 tbsp	extra virgin olive oil	15 mL
$^1/_2$ cup	diced onion	120 mL
$2^1/_2$ cups	Arborio rice, *FIOR DI RISO*	600 mL
$^3/_4$ cup	white wine	180 mL
24	large prawns 26/30, peeled	24
GARNISH		
	truffle oil (optional) (see p. 27)	
$^1/_3$ cup	fresh parsley, finely minced	80 mL

SERVES 6–8

Prepare roasted garlic and crispy shallots and set aside.

In a large pot, bring the stock to a low simmer. Maintain this simmer during the entire cooking process. In a larger pot, heat the butter and olive oil together, add the onion and sauté until it is soft. Stir in the rice and continue to cook on medium heat until the rice turns opaque. Pour in the wine, stirring until it is almost absorbed.

Ladle the simmering stock into the rice pot $^1/_2$ cup (120 mL) at a time. Wait until each addition is almost completely absorbed before adding the next $^1/_2$ cup (120 mL). Stir continuously to prevent the rice from sticking and gumming up.

Add the prawns to the rice after about 20 minutes of cooking or when the rice is almost cooked through. When the prawns begin to turn pink, add the roasted garlic and crispy shallots. Continue to cook, adding the remaining stock and stirring until the rice is fully cooked.

Serve immediately. A light touch of truffle oil is a great optional finish, garnish with the minced parsley.

CAREN'S ADVICE

Prawns are measured by quantity in a pound. When a recipe calls for 26/30, it means that 26 to 30 prawns equal one pound. This is the size we use most frequently. Stepping up for special dinners, 21/25s indicate a larger size and 36/40 will mean very small shrimp. It's your call, now you know.

You might see the letters IQF on packages of frozen prawns. IQF relates to frozen product that is individually and not block frozen.

Wild Mushroom Risotto

Risotto is comfort food like no other. This creamy brilliant cooking method, perfected by the Milanese, has embraced and held restaurant-goers captive forever. Risotto, because of the long stirring method required, is not a home-friendly recipe for many people. If you can overcome the time factor and total attention this rice dish requires, you too can master this northern Italian classic.

1 cup	dried wild mushrooms, such as cèpes, porcini, morels, *PLANTIN*	240 mL
5–6 cups	chicken, vegetable or beef stock, hot	1.2–1.5 L
3 tbsp	unsalted butter	45 mL
1/2 cup	medium yellow onion, finely diced	1/2
2 cups	Arborio rice, *FIOR DI RISO* preferably a canaroli	480 mL
1/2 cup	dry white wine	120 mL
to taste	sea salt	
to taste	freshly ground tellicherry or black pepper	
2 tbsp	unsalted butter	30 mL
1/2 cup	freshly grated Parmesan cheese	120 mL
	drizzle of truffle oil (optional) (see p. 27)	

SERVES 6

Place the dried mushrooms in a large bowl and cover completely with hot water. Let them sit for at least 30 minutes, then squeeze out most of their liquid and chop. In a large pot, bring the stock to a low simmer. Maintain this simmer during the entire cooking process.

Place the butter and the onion in a heavy-bottomed pot, with the heat on medium. Cook the onion until it is soft but not brown. Add the rice to the pot and cook until it becomes translucent. This will take 3–5 minutes. Once the rice is translucent, add the wine all at once. Stir the rice until the wine has been absorbed. Begin adding the hot stock a 1/2 cup (120 mL) at a time, stirring all the while, until the stock is absorbed. Then add another cup of stock and proceed to stir in the same manner until the stock is absorbed again.

When you are halfway through the stock, add the soaked chopped mushrooms. Pour the soaking liquid into the stock pot. Continue adding the stock and stirring until the rice is cooked to your liking. It should be cooked al dente—still firm, but not mushy.

To finish the dish, season with sea salt, freshly ground pepper, the remaining butter and Parmesan cheese. Just before serving the risotto, lightly drizzle truffle oil over top.

CAREN'S ADVICE

When choosing an Arborio rice, quality is the defining factor. I like Fior di Riso for its ability to stand up without becoming gummy.

When purchasing truffle oil, buy "infused" not "flavored," white and not black. In both cases the intensity in flavor and aroma is far superior. Truffle paste takes the flavor dimension of truffle as far as you can—well, except that of fresh. My prefence is La Madia Regale.

Joyce's Duck and Mushroom Risotto
with Cilantro Lime Jelly

Joyce Ross attended my cooking school for many years. It always inspired me when she and her girlfriends arrived at the school with tremendous enthusiasm. A stroke of luck occurred as we chatted in my store one day. I said, "You're here so much you should work here." She said, "Okay," and our already good team got better. She also cooks well and this is one of her personal bests.

5 cups	chicken stock, *MAJOR*	1.2 L
1/4 cup	unsalted butter	60 mL
1	large onion, diced	1
1 1/2 cups	Arborio rice, *FIOR DI RISO*	360 mL
3 cups	button mushrooms, sautéed and sliced	720 mL
8	scallops, or	8
1 1/2 cups	duck, cooked and shredded	360 mL
2 tbsp	butter	30 mL
	truffle oil (see p. 27)	
to taste	sea salt and pepper	

GARNISH

cilantro lime or red pepper jelly, warmed

fresh cilantro sprigs

SERVES 6

In a large pot, heat the stock and keep it at medium heat during the entire cooking process.

In a heavy-bottomed pot, melt the butter, add the onions until soft. Add the rice and stir over medium heat until translucent. Once the rice is translucent, add the stock 1/2 cup (120 mL) at a time, continuing to stir until the liquid is absorbed before adding the next 1/2 cup (120 mL). Continue until the rice is cooked and tender.

While the rice is cooking, cook the scallops in butter for about 2–4 minutes or warm the cooked and shredded duck by sautéing it in the butter. Set aside.

To serve, use cooking rings. Mound the cooked risotto inside the ring, add a few drops of truffle oil, then top with the duck. Brush the top with warmed jelly and a sprig of cilantro.

CAREN'S ADVICE

To make your life easy, purchase your cooked duck at a good Chinese take-out store or deli.

Moroccan Lamb in Pita Pockets

If food could be cute, this recipe would have more dimples than you could handle. I use mini pita breads, open them and stuff the bottom with onion jam, then thinly sliced grilled lamb. If red meat isn't your thing, use chicken, fish or stir-fried veggies. This is one of my favorites.

3/4 tsp	freshly ground nutmeg	4 mL
1/4 tsp	ground cloves	1.2 mL
1 tsp	ground tellicherry or Malabar pepper	5 mL
1 tsp	ground white pepper	5 mL
1 1/2 tsp	ground cinnamon	7.5 mL
2 tsp	ground cardamom	10 mL
1/4 tsp	cayenne	1.2 mL
1/4 tsp	cumin	1.2 mL
1/4 tsp	turmeric	1.2 mL
1/2 tsp	fleur de sel (see p. 25)	2.5 mL
ONION JAM		
3 tbsp	olive oil or butter	45 mL
5	large white onions, peeled and sliced	5
1/3 cup	brown sugar	80 mL
1/3 cup	balsamic vinegar	80 mL
1/3 cup	port wine	80 mL
2 lb	trimmed lamb loin	900 g
2 tbsp	extra virgin olive oil	30 mL
SAUCE		
1 cup	Balkan style yogurt	240 mL
1/2	lemon, juice of	1/2
1 tsp	ground cardamom	5 mL
1 pkg	mini pita breads (12 per pkg)	1 pkg

MAKES ABOUT 12 PITAS — SERVES 6

Mix the nutmeg, cloves, pepper, cinnamon, cardamom, cayenne, cumin, turmeric and fleur de sel together and set aside.

For the onion jam, heat a large nonstick fry pan to medium and add the butter or oil. Add the white onions and fry until they begin to turn dark golden brown. When they are evenly brown, add the brown sugar, balsamic vinegar and port wine. Let the onion mixture simmer until most of the liquid is absorbed. It will be the consistency of a thick jam. Set aside until serving. This can be made up to 4 days ahead and chilled.

Pat the lamb dry. Rub the seasoning spices into the lamb making sure that you cover all surfaces. Heat a fry pan to medium high heat. Add 2 tbsp (30 mL) olive oil. Sauté the lamb on all sides until it is done to your preference. Remove from heat and let rest for about 5 minutes. Slice thin. Prepare the yogurt sauce.

Open the small pita pockets, add a generous tbsp of onion jam, then the sliced lamb and a dollop of the yogurt sauce. Serve warm or at room temperature. I like to wrap the bottoms in tin foil squares for a picnic look.

CAREN'S ADVICE

As a guide to working with lamb, an internal temperature of 140°F (60°C) is rare, 160°F (71°C) is medium.

Mexican Quesadillas with a Twist

The first time I met Jill Krop she was late for our first Saturday morning chef segment on Global TV. Racing into the cooking school, with make-up in hand and donning her news anchor suit jacket, she introduced herself, "I'm Jill Krop. No, I don't drink coffee thanks and what are we cooking?"

That was many years ago. She has since moved up in TV news land. We have, however, become great friends over the years. As Mexico is one of her true loves, here are two recipes from her many travels there.

3 cups	cooked black beans	720 mL
6	8-inch (20-cm) flour tortillas (any flavor but I prefer the plain ones)	6
1	mango, sliced	1
1 lb	feta cheese, crumbled	450 g

MAKES 6 QUESADILLAS

Spread the black beans over the entire tortilla. Cover one half in sliced mango and small chunks of feta cheese. Fold in half and either cook in a lightly oiled frying pan until both sides are golden, or bake at 350°F (180°C) for 10 minutes for fewer calories! This combination is classically Mexican with a tangy twist. If you don't like feta, use Monterey Jack cheese or even mozzarella for a different flavor.

Show-Off Quesadillas

These tortillas take a little extra effort in the preparation, but the end result is quite delicious and if you're not really a "chef," your friends will be very impressed!

3	large red potatoes	3
to taste	lime juice	
to taste	salt (preferably sel de mer)	
to taste	freshly ground tellicherry or black pepper	
2	large onions, caramelized	3
splash	of extra virgin olive oil	
pinch	of sugar	
1 lb	Monterey Jack cheese, grated	450 g
6	8-inch (20-cm) flour tortillas	6

MAKES 6 QUESADILLAS

Thinly slice several small red potatoes. Lay on a greased cookie sheet and season with fresh lime juice, salt and pepper. Bake until al dente, or soft if you prefer them that way.

Slice up the onions and sauté them in some olive oil and sugar until they caramelize. Shred the Monterey Jack cheese.

Layer the potatoes, onions and cheese on half a tortilla. If you want, you can spread black beans on the tortilla for a slightly moister quesadilla. Fold and cook as in the previous recipe.

Buen provecho!

Pesto Pull Aparts

I have taken a basic bread dough, rolled it out and spread pesto over top. The fragrant, pungent and very friendly flavor of basil makes this simple recipe a perfect accompaniment for any soup or salad that wants a homemade touch.

1 tsp	sugar	5 mL
1/2 cup	warm water	120 mL
1 tbsp	yeast	15 mL
2	large eggs	2
1/4 cup	buttermilk	60 mL
2 cups	unbleached all-purpose flour	480 mL
1/2 cup	jarred pesto sauce, *ITALIA IN TAVOLA*	120 mL

SERVES 6

Stir the sugar into the water and sprinkle the yeast over top. Let this sit until the mixture begins to bubble. Lightly beat together the eggs and buttermilk. Set aside. Place the flour in a bowl fitted with a dough hook. Add the proofed yeast and egg mixture. Beat on medium speed until the dough is mixed. Remove from the bowl and hand knead for 2–3 minutes or until the dough is smooth and elastic. Lightly oil the dough and place in a bowl until it has doubled in size—about 40 minutes.

Grease an 8 x 8 inch (20 x 20 cm) baking pan. Place the dough on a lightly floured surface and roll out to 12 x 17 inch (30 x 43 cm). Spread the surface with the pesto. Roll up jelly roll fashion and cut into 1/2-inch (1.2-cm) rolls. Place rolls cut side up in the prepared pan and let rise for another 30 minutes. Preheat oven to 400°F (200°C) and bake for about 30–45 minutes or until golden brown.

Napa Valley Wine Auction launch dinner. Talk about nerves and heat. Bob Lawrence, me and Diane Lawrence

Fig and Shallot Focaccia

An incredible bread that can go with any meal or stand solo in the bread basket.

5	large shallots, sliced thin	5
1 tbsp	unbleached all-purpose flour	15 mL
4 tbsp	olive oil	60 mL
1 1/2 cup	Black Mission figs, chopped, hot water to cover	250 mL
1 tsp	sugar	5 mL
3/4 cup	warm water	180 mL
1 tbsp	instant dry yeast	15 mL
4–5 cups	unbleached all-purpose flour	950 mL–1.2 L
1 3/4 cup	warm water	420 mL
2 tbsp	olive oil	30 mL
1 tbsp	sea salt	15 mL
2–3 tbsp	olive oil for brushing dough	30–45 mL
1–2 tbsp	coarse sea salt	15–30 mL
1 tbsp	coarsely cracked black pepper	15 mL

SERVES 6–8

Toss the sliced shallots in the flour, shake off and discard the excess flour. Heat the oil in a small fry pan and sauté the shallots until golden brown. Drain on paper towel and set aside.

Place the figs in a bowl, cover with very hot water and let them sit for 10 minutes to soften. Drain well and set aside.

Dissolve the sugar in the warm water, add the yeast and let it rest until mixture begins to bubble. Place 4 cups (960 mL) of the flour in a large mixing bowl fitted with a dough hook. If you don't have a mixer, place the flour in a large bowl and proceed in the same manner.

Add the water, oil, salt and proofed yeast. Mix lightly until the dough begins to come together. Add the reserved shallots and figs. Add the remaining 1 cup (240 mL) of flour a little at a time until a smooth elastic dough is achieved. Place in a lightly oiled bowl and cover until doubled in size.

Punch down and turn out onto an oiled cookie sheet with 1-inch (2.5-cm) sides. Press the dough evenly into the corners. Brush with 2–3 tbsp (30–45 mL) of olive oil and sprinkle with the coarse sea salt and black pepper.

Preheat oven to 400°F (200°C). Let rise for 30 minutes, then bake for 20 minutes or until browned. Cut into squares and serve.

Wild Rice Pancakes

These great little pancakes can certainly stand proud as a substitute for potatoes. You can also make them bite-sized as an appetizer—top with grilled prawns, smoked salmon or duck. The only thing holding you back is lack of imagination.

2	eggs, separate yolks and whites	2
2 cups	unbleached flour	480 mL
1 tsp	sea salt	5 mL
3 tsp	baking powder	15 ml
2 cups	fully cooked wild rice, well drained	480 mL
to taste	freshly ground tellicherry or black pepper	
2 cups	buttermilk	480 mL

SERVES 6

Beat the egg whites until soft peaks form, set aside.

Sift the flour, salt and baking powder into a large bowl. Add in the cooked rice and toss to coat. Season with pepper to taste

Whisk the yolks and add to the buttermilk. Pour over the rice/flour mixture and stir. Fold in the reserved egg whites. Pour the batter into small pancakes on a hot greased skillet. Cook on both sides until golden.

CAREN'S ADVICE

Wild rice is really not rice at all. It is harvested from long-grain marsh grasses in Manitoba and the northern Great Lakes. 1 cup (240 mL) of un-cooked rice yields 3 cups (720 mL) cooked. Unlike rice, this seed can take up to 1 hour to cook.

Michelle Corday
BC Child Charity Fundraiser

Cheese Bread

The cuteness of the terra cotta flower pots makes this bread unique. If the pots aren't your thing, use basic bread pans they've worked forever. Remember, yeast is just an ingredient, don't turn the page!

¹/₄ cup	milk	60 mL
1 tsp	sugar	5 mL
1 tbsp	yeast	15 mL
2 cups	unbleached all-purpose flour	475 mL
to taste	sea salt	
to taste	grounded 5 blend peppercorns	
3	large eggs, beaten	3
¹/₄ cup	unsalted butter, at room temperature	60 mL
1 cup	Swiss Gruyère cheese, cubed	240 mL
	butter for greasing pots	
1	egg, lightly beaten, mixed with 1 tsp (5 mL) salt for glaze	1

MAKES 4 4-INCH (10-CM) LOAVES OR POTS

You will need 4 terra cotta pots 4-inches (10 cm) in diameter. Use new ones and immerse in water for 1 hour before using. Heat the milk and sugar together until just tepid (as warm as a baby bottle). Sprinkle the yeast over and let it begin to bubble—in about 5 minutes.

Combine the flour, sea salt and pepper in a large bowl. Make a well in the center and add the proofed yeast, beaten eggs and butter. Mix together, making a nice soft dough. Add the cheese and distribute evenly.

Cover with a cloth and let the dough rise for about one hour or until doubled in size.

Grease the pots well with butter. When the dough has doubled, lightly punch it down. Divide it into four portions and place them into the prepared pots. Let the dough rise again until it has doubled in size.

Brush the top of the dough with the egg glaze and bake at 375°F (190°C) for 30–40 minutes, depending on the size of the pan. The bread is cooked when it sounds hollow when tapped.

Pita Crisps

These rustic little crisps can double as a cracker for any dip or spread. They are simple, quick and make a perfect mate when placed alongside hummus (see p. 34).

1 pkg	8-inch (20-cm) pita bread	1
¹/₂ cup	extra virgin olive oil	120 mL

MAKES 6 DOZEN PIECES

Split the pita bread in half. Cut into wedges of 4 or 6. Lightly brush with oil and place in a single layer on an ungreased cookie sheet. Bake at 325°F (165°C) for about 8–10 minutes or until crisp and light golden brown. Store in an airtight container. They keep for about 7–10 days.

Picnic Sandwiches

This is a great addition to a picnic, or simply a lunch favorite. For your carnivorous friends, add a few slices of prosciutto or mortadella to make the sandwich complete.

1	zucchini, thinly sliced	1
	olive oil to brush	
1	ciabatta	1
1–2 tsp	olive oil to drizzle	15–30 mL
3/4 cup	tapenade (olive paste), *ARNAUD*	180 mL
2	roasted red peppers (jarred variety is fine), sliced	2
8	slices provolone or Swiss cheese	8
1	big bunch arugula, washed and dried	1

SERVES 6

Slice the zucchini lengthwise, brush with a little olive oil and grill 1–2 minutes each side until cooked but still firm. Cut the ciabatta down the middle and drizzle both sides with a little olive oil. Spread both sides with the tapenade.

Layer the roasted peppers, grilled zucchini, cheese and arugula, on one half of the bread. Top with the other bread half. Wrap tightly with plastic wrap. Lay a heavy weight on top to press the bread down. Let the sandwich sit under the weight for at least 30 minutes.

Remove the plastic wrap, cut into 3–4 inch (7.5 cm–10 cm) slices, wrap securely with parchment paper or brown wrapping paper and tie with brown string. Tuck a fresh herb sprig under the string for garnish.

CAREN'S ADVICE

I use a quality jarred tapenade like Arnaud. Whether you use black or green olives is your choice. "Ciabatta" is Italian for slipper, named because of this bread's flat slipper shape.

Pecan Sticky Buns

Please do not let the word yeast facilitate the turning of this page. As easy as baking powder is to add to dry ingredients, such can be said of yeast. The singular significant difference is dissolving the yeast in water. The results are not only worth the wait but crowd pleasing. Go forth, all of you wannabe dough punchers.

LIQUID

1 cup	milk	240 mL
1/4 cup	unsalted butter	115 g
1 tsp	sea salt	5 mL
1/2 cup	sugar	120 mL

YEAST MIXTURE

1 tsp	sugar	5 mL
1 cup	warm water	240 mL
2 tbsp	yeast	30 mL

DOUGH

6 cups	unbleached all-purpose flour	1.5 L
1	lemon, zest of	1
2	large eggs, lightly beaten	2

PAN PREPARATION

1/2 cup	soft unsalted butter	120 mL
3/4 cup	brown sugar	180 mL
1 cup	pecans, coarsely chopped	240 mL

FILLING

1/2 lb	soft unsalted butter	225 g
1 cup	brown sugar	240 mL
1 tbsp	ground cinnamon	15 mL

MAKES 24 BUNS

LIQUID

Place the milk, butter, salt and sugar in a small saucepan. Heat on low just until the butter melts and the sugar dissolves. Set aside to cool.

YEAST MIXTURE

Stir the sugar into the warm water and sprinkle the yeast on top. Let it sit until it begins to bubble—about 5 minutes.

DOUGH

Place 3 cups (750 mL) of the flour in a large mixing bowl fitted with a dough hook. Add the cooled milk mixture, proofed yeast, zest and beaten eggs to the bowl. Mix on low until all the flour incorporates into the liquid. Add the remaining flour a cup at a time, mixing well after each addition. Turn the dough out onto a lightly floured
surface and hand knead until it becomes smooth and elastic.

Lightly butter the top of the dough and place in a bowl, letting it rise until it doubles in size, about 2 hours. Transfer the dough to a floured surface and roll into an 18 x 21 inch (46 x 53 cm) rectangle.

PAN PREPARATION

Spread the butter into two pans: one 9 x 13 inch (23 x 23 cm) and one 8-inch (20-cm) round pan. Sprinkle evenly with brown sugar and pecans. Set aside until the dough is ready.

FILLING

Using your hands spread the soft butter evenly over the surface of the dough. Top with the brown sugar and cinnamon. Roll the dough up jelly roll fashion and cut into 24 1-inch (2.5-cm) slices. Place the slices cut side up into the prepared pans.

Let the buns rise for one hour.

Bake in a preheated 350°F (175°C) oven for 25–30 minutes or until golden brown. Invert, while still warm, onto a large platter.

Raisin French Toast

The perfect breakfast food, the brunch menu pick, and—when prepared in this decadent manner—a fast favorite for everyone. Cream cheese can jump in as mascarpone's substitute if she is out of town!

1	loaf raisin bread (unsliced)	1
8 oz	mascarpone cheese (room temperature)	227 mL
4	large eggs, lightly beaten	4
1/2 cup	light cream	120 mL
1 tsp	pure vanilla extract	5 mL
1 tbsp	brandy, optional	15 mL
1/2 tsp	cinnamon	2.5 mL
	grating of fresh nutmeg	
	unsalted butter for frying	
	maple syrup	

SERVES 6–8

Slice the bread into 1/2-inch (1.2-cm) thick pieces. Spread 2 tbsp (30 mL) of the mascarpone on one slice and sandwich with a second slice of bread. Beat the remaining ingredients together, dip the bread slices into the egg batter and fry until lightly golden adding more butter as needed for frying.

Serve with real maple syrup.

CAREN'S ADVICE

I believe that nasty supermarket vanillas, bearing names such as "pure imitation," should never make their way into your cupboard, let alone your baked goods. You are better off using nothing.

Jack Stoughton, Umberto Menghi and me

Zucchini and Carrot Muffins

Muffins, muffins, muffins! They can be good, bad or downright nasty, it depends completely on the recipe. These are very good muffins, thanks to the creator, Diane Lawrence. I think the best part is the cream cheese center, although picking at the toasted pecan top is also quite enjoyable. Add a cappuccino and enjoy!

$^{1}/_{2}$ cup	unsalted butter	120 mL
$^{3}/_{4}$ cup	sugar	180 mL
2	large eggs	2
1	orange, zest of	1
2 cups	unbleached flour	480 mL
$1^{1}/_{2}$ tsp	baking powder	7.5 mL
$1^{1}/_{2}$ tsp	baking soda	7.5 mL
$^{1}/_{4}$ tsp	ground cloves	1.2 mL
$^{1}/_{4}$ tsp	ground nutmeg	1.2 mL
$1^{1}/_{2}$ cups	raw carrots, shredded	360 mL
$^{1}/_{2}$ cup	raw zucchini, shredded	120 mL
$^{1}/_{3}$ cup	orange juice or water	80 mL
1 cup	raisins, preferably organic	240 mL
1 (8 oz)	pkg firm cream cheese	1 (227 mL)
$^{1}/_{2}$ cup	toasted pecans	120 mL

MAKES 12 MUFFINS

Cream the butter and sugar together, beating until light and fluffy. Add the eggs one at a time, beating well after each addition. Add the orange zest.

In a separate bowl, sift together the flour, baking powder, baking soda, cloves and nutmeg. Add half of the flour mix to the butter mixture, then fold in the carrots, zucchini and juice or water. Add the remaining flour mixture and raisins.

Grease 12 muffin cups. Half-fill with batter. Spoon one heaping tbsp of the cream cheese on top of the batter. Spoon over enough batter to cover the cream cheese completely.

Top each muffin with a few pecans. Bake at 350°F (175°C) for 35–45 minutes.

Pauline Jones
(my very first sôus-chef)

Margaret Cook's Scones

My dear friend Susan Meister, owner of Fabulous Foods Catering, was blessed with a Scottish mother. Her scones are like no other. The texture is silky and the taste makes your mouth water. The only improvement comes with generous dollops of Devon cream and homemade preserves.

2 cups	unbleached all-purpose flour	480 mL
4 tsp	baking powder	20 mL
	pinch of sea salt	
1/2 cup	unsalted butter	120 mL
1	large egg, lightly beaten	1
1/2 cup	whipping cream	120 mL
1/4 cup	sugar (for sprinkling)	60 mL
ADD-ON OPTIONS		
2/3 cup	fresh blueberries	160 mL
1/2 cup	dried currants	120 mL
1 tsp	orange zest	5 mL
2/3 cup	dried cranberries	160 mL
1 cup	aged cheddar cheese, cubed	240 mL

MAKES 8 LARGE SCONES

Preheat oven to 400°F (200°C). Sift the flour, baking powder and salt into a large bowl. Using a dough blender, cut the butter into the dry ingredients until the mixture is the size of large peas. Set aside.

Add the lightly beaten egg to the cream, then pour into the butter/flour mixture. Add in any of the options at this point, if desired. Gather and mix the dough together, being careful not to overmix.

Roll out to about 1 inch (2.5 cm) thick. Cut into wedges or use a cookie cutter to stamp out your shape. Transfer the scones to a silicone sheet or parchment-lined cookie sheet and sprinkle the tops lightly with some sugar. Bake for 12–18 minutes or until golden brown.

Serve warm with butter and jam.

entrées

Curried Vegetable Strudel

What a way to enjoy veggies! This recipe was actually created by virtue of leftovers—leftover stir fry and half a package of filo pastry. I have a love for curry but if you don't, simply substitute a cheese sauce.

¹/₄ cup	grapeseed or vegetable oil	60 mL
4 cups	mixed vegetables: onion, broccoli, celery, carrot, mushrooms, snow peas, cauliflower,etc.	950 mL
2	garlic cloves, minced	2
1 inch	piece of fresh ginger, grated	2.5 cm
1¹/₂ cups	Curry Sauce (see p. 178)	360 mL
2 cups	cooked rice, basmati or jasmine	480 mL
1 cup	Monterey Jack or mozzarella cheese, grated	240 mL
¹/₂ cup	fresh cilantro, chopped	120 mL
8 oz pkg	filo pastry (¹/₂ pkg)	225 g
	oil for brushing the filo	
¹/₂ cup	Parmesan cheese, grated	120 mL

MAKES 2 STRUDELS/SERVES 6–8

Heat a wok to high and add the oil and veggies. Stir fry for about 1 minute. Add the garlic and ginger. Continue to stir fry until the veggies are about ³/₄ cooked. Transfer to a large bowl and cool.

Stir the Curry Sauce into the veggies. Add the rice, grated cheese and cilantro and mix to combine. Set aside.

On your work surface, lay out the filo pastry for one strudel. Lightly brush one sheet with oil and then lightly sprinkle Parmesan cheese on top. Repeat with layers of pastry, oil and cheese for about 7 layers.

Take half of the vegetable mixture and lay it on the filo. Roll the pastry up, tucking in the ends.

Repeat process to make second strudel with remaining pastry.

Place on a cookie sheet, lightly brush the tops with oil and gently score knife marks on the tops of the filos. Be careful to penetrate only the top 3 layers. This is just for visual effect.

Bake at 400°F (200°C) for about 15 minutes, or until the filos are light golden brown. Serve in slices with a little extra Curry Sauce on the side.

Who would have guess it's the urban peasant? James Barber and me, we must be 15!

Quick Veggie Chili

This recipe was created in the desperation of time and the need for flavorful comfort food. The misery of wet winter weather helped feed the need for this gutsy meatless chili.

3 tbsp	extra virgin olive oil	45 mL
1	large onion, diced	1
2	carrots, diced	2
1	celery stalk, diced	1
1	medium turnip, peeled and diced	1
2–3	garlic cloves, minced	2–3
2 tbsp	hot chili powder (less if desired)	30 mL
1 tsp	ground cumin	5 mL
1/4 tsp	ground cinnamon	1.2 mL
1 tbsp	smoked Spanish paprika, *LA CHINATA* (more if desired)	15 mL
1 (28 oz)	can whole Italian plum tomatoes with juice	1 (796 mL)
1 (14 oz)	can black turtle beans	1 (398 mL)
1 (14 oz)	can red kidney beans	1 (398 mL)
1	bay leaf	1
1/2 cup	fresh cilantro, chopped	120 mL
to taste	sea salt	

GARNISH

1/2 lb	freshly grated Monterey Jack	225 g

SERVES 6

CAREN'S ADVICE

I use scissors to cut canned tomatoes into pieces. It leaves you no mess to clean up and all the pieces are even.

Heat the oil in a deep soup pot, add the onion and cook until it begins to brown. Add the carrots, celery and turnip. Continue to sauté for about 10 minutes, or until the veggies begin to soften. Add the garlic and continue to sauté.

Sprinkle the chili, cumin, cinnamon and Spanish paprika over the vegetables and continue to cook for about 2 minutes. Using scissors, cut the tomatoes into pieces and add to the pot along with the juice. Stir to combine the mixture, add both cans of beans and the bay leaf and let the chili simmer, uncovered, for at least 30 minutes.

Just before serving, stir in the cilantro and season to taste. Ladle into ovenproof bowls and spread a generous layer of grated Monterey Jack cheese over top. Place the bowls under the broiler and grill until the cheese is bubbly and golden brown.

Crusty Italian bread, or any of the bread recipes in this book, and, of course, a bottle of Zinfandel, would marry quite well with this.

Spanish Paella

This is a recipe for a party! It serves 10–12 generously. I always find when I entertain large numbers, one-dish meals work the best. Paella is one such crowd pleaser. You can cut the recipe in half for smaller, more intimate dinners.

1 cup	olive oil	240 mL
20	chicken thighs, skin removed	20
1 lb	spicy chorizo sausage, sliced	455 g
2	large yellow onions, diced	2
4–6	large garlic cloves, minced	4–6
1	large yellow pepper, diced	1
1	large red pepper, diced	1
4 cups	long grain white rice	950 mL
2 tbsp	smoked Spanish paprika, *LA CHINATA*	30 mL
2	bay leaves	2
2 tsp	saffron threads	10 mL
1/2 cup	white wine	120 mL
8 cups	chicken stock	2 L
24	prawns	24
24	littleneck clams	24
24	mussels, beards removed	24
1 cup	frozen baby peas	240 mL

GARNISH

3	lemons, sliced into wedges and edge dipped into paprika	3
	parsley, finely chopped	

SERVES 10–12

Heat 1/2 cup (120 mL) of the oil in a large ovenproof skillet, add the chicken thighs and fry until almost cooked through, about 20 minutes. Remove and set aside. Add the chorizo to the pan and brown well, remove and add to the chicken. Wipe the pan clean with paper towels.

Heat the remaining 1/2 cup (120 mL) of oil, sauté the onion, garlic and both peppers until soft and lightly browned. Add the rice to the pan and stir to combine. Add the paprika, bay leaves, saffron, wine and stock. Bring to a boil, add the reserved chicken and chorizo, cover and transfer to a preheated 400°F (200°C) oven for about 15 minutes. Turn the heat down to 350°F (175°C), add the prawns, clams, mussels and peas. Bake a further 10–15 minutes or until the rice is cooked and the shellfish open. Discard any mussels or prawns that do not open.

Garnish the dish with the lemon wedges and finely chopped parsley.

CAREN'S ADVICE

When saffron is called for in a recipe, place the threads in a mortar and pestle together with a teaspoon (5 mL) of salt and pound into a powder. Add to any liquid in your recipe to maximize the flavor. Luis Ayala Miralles is my choice.

Cataplana

A cataplana is indispensable to a Portuguese kitchen. The clam-shaped copper steamer is not only the cooking vessel but also the serving dish. When opened at the table it dramatically releases the fabulous aroma of its contents. A large pot with a tight lid can be substituted. The traditional version of cataplana does not include mussels or prawns, but living on the west coast of Canada inspired me to add them for local flavor.

1 lb	chorizo sausage, sliced	455 g
1/4 cup	extra virgin olive oil	60 mL
2	medium yellow onions, diced	2
3	garlic cloves, minced	3
2 cups	plum tomatoes, chopped	480 mL
1 cup	white wine	240 mL
1	green pepper, diced	1
1	bunch fresh parsley, chopped	1
to taste	sea salt	
to taste	freshly ground pepper	
to taste	piri piri sauce (see p. 54) or Tabasco	
24	manila or littleneck clams in shells	24
24	mussels in shells	24
12	prawns in shells	12
1/4 cup	brandy	60 mL
6 cups	cooked rice	1.5 L

SERVES 6–8

Fry the chopped chorizo sausage until crisp. Set aside.

In a cataplana dish, heat the olive oil. Add the onion and garlic and cook until soft but not brown. Add the tomatoes, wine, green pepper, parsley, salt, pepper and piri piri sauce or Tabasco sauce to taste.

Bring to a boil, stirring frequently. Add the clams, mussels, prawns and brandy. Cover and cook for about 5 minutes. Discard any unopened shells.

Serve cataplana over rice with the chorizo as your garnish.

The Portugese are cooking! What a dinner. Tivoli Hotel chef, José Valagao, Tivoli Hotel chef, Ruy Paes-Braga and me

Halibut on Lemon Grass Sticks

The lemon grass sticks provide a unique way to serve the halibut. If lemon grass is unavailable use metal skewers or proceed without cubing the fish. Alternatively, prawns or scallops work very well as a substitute for halibut.

MARINADE

6 tbsp	Balkan-style yogurt	90 mL
4 tbsp	fresh lemon juice	60 mL
1 tsp	smoked Spanish paprika, *LA CHINATA*	5 mL
1/2 tsp	ground cumin	2.5 mL
1 tsp	garam masala	5 mL
1 tsp	fresh ginger, minced	5 mL
2	fresh garlic cloves, minced	2
to taste	sea salt	
to taste	freshly ground pepper, preferably malabar or tellicherry	
2 tbsp	grapeseed oil	30 mL
1/2 tsp	ground cardamom	2.5 mL
2 lb	halibut fillets, cut into 2-inch (5-cm) cubes	900 g
3	bunches lemon grass (see p. 17)	3

GARNISH

lime wedges

MAKES 12 SKEWERS/SERVES 6

MARINADE

Mix together all of the ingredients, except for the halibut and lemon grass. Stir well to combine. Add the halibut to the marinade, stirring to ensure that it is coated evenly. Cover and chill for 30 minutes.

Trim the lemon grass and peel back until you have just the stiff center left. Cut into lengths of about 5 inches (12.5 cm). When the fish has marinated, thread 3 pieces on each lemon grass stick.

Heat a ribbed griddle to high heat and brush on a little oil. Grill the skewered halibut on both sides for about 2 minutes each side or until cooked through. Serve on a platter garnished with lime wedges.

CAREN'S ADVICE

Grapeseed oil is a favorite with me when a flavorless oil is required. It not only lets the flavors of the food shine, but provides a smoke point for frying.

West Coast Halibut Cheeks

Halibut cheeks are undeniably my favorite part of the fish. The approach of spring brings these fabulous cheeks to market. They are moist and succulent and can be interchanged with any fish in your favorite fish recipes. I urge you to try them—if fish could be addicitive, then cheeks would do it.

2$^{1}/_{2}$ lbs	fresh halibut cheeks	1.125 kg
$^{1}/_{3}$ cup	unbleached all-purpose flour	80 mL
2 tbsp	extra virgin olive oil	30 mL
2 tbsp	unsalted butter	30 mL
3	shallots, finely minced	3
3 tbsp	flat-leaf parsley, chopped	45 mL
1 tbsp	capers	15 mL
2 tsp	chopped fresh thyme	10 mL
$^{2}/_{3}$ cup	white wine	160 mL
to taste	sea salt	
to taste	freshly ground white pepper	

SERVES 6

Dredge the halibut cheeks in the flour. Heat the oil and butter together in a fry pan, add the halibut cheeks and cook until golden brown, about 2–3 minutes on each side. Add the shallots, parsley, capers and thyme. Continue to cook for 4 more minutes.

Add the wine to the pan along with the salt and white pepper and cook until the cheeks are cooked through. Depending on the size of the cheeks, this may be another minute or so. Serve the cheeks with steamed baby potatoes or your favorite vegetable, and ladle the pan juices over top.

Jill Krop and Kevin Newman at our annual BC Child Charity Fundraiser

Tequi-Lime™ BBQ Salmon
with Mango and Red Pepper Salsa

Ann Kirsebom is the creator of this delicious Tequila Lime Marinade. A caterer by profession, her passion and creativity produced this remarkable marinade. I have used it on chicken, salmon and ribs. Quite honestly, if only one marinade found its way into my kitchen, it would be this one.

6	5 oz (140 g) salmon fillets	6
³/₄ cup	Tequi-Lime™ BBQ sauce	180 mL

MANGO SALSA

1	fresh mango, peeled and diced	1
1	red pepper, diced	1
1 tbsp	juice of lime, freshly squeezed	15 mL
2–3 tsp	white sugar (to taste)	15–45 mL

SERVES 6

Marinate salmon fillets in the Tequi-Lime™ BBQ sauce in the refrigerator for 1–2 hours prior to cooking.

While salmon is marinating, prepare the Mango Salsa by combining all ingredients. Set aside.

Grill salmon, basting frequently with additional sauce (presentation side first—skin up) for about 2 minutes over a high heat. Turn on an angle to achieve grill marks for about 2 minutes. Flip over and finish grilling, about another minute. Do not over cook as the salmon will continue to cook when it is removed from the grill. Serve with room temperature Mango Salsa.

Skate Wings

My husband José is a Portuguese national. If you have ever visited Portugal, you will know that the food of choice is always fish. In our house he is the master of fish cookery. I attribute this talent to salt cod running in his veins. He says that it is simply his culinary talents. Although skate is not a commonly cooked fish because of the cartilage, I urge you to try it. It is quick to prepare and well worth asking for in your fish market.

¹/3 cup	olive oil	80 mL
2 tbsp	unsalted butter	30 mL
2¹/2 lb	fresh skate wings	1.1 kg
2 tbsp	capers	30 mL
¹/2 cup	white wine	120 mL
1	lemon, juice of	1
to taste	sea salt	
to taste	white pepper	

GARNISH
¹/3 cup	fresh cilantro, chopped	80 mL

SERVES 4

Preheat oven to 350°F (175°C). Heat the oil and butter in a large ovenproof fry pan, add the skate wings and brown on both sides, about 5 minutes. Add the capers and wine. Transfer the entire pan to the oven for about 12 minutes. The fish will fall from the bone when ready.

Remove from the oven, add the lemon juice, sea salt and pepper to taste. Cook for about 1 more minute and garnish with the chopped cilantro. Roasted potatoes and grilled vegetables make this dinner complete.

Sesame-Crusted Tuna
with Wasabi Sauce

When something tastes this good, it's usually extremely difficult to believe that it's actually simple and quick. I have this saying that is used often when Bill Good and I talk food Thursdays on CKNW/98: If you can read, you can cook. This recipe exemplifies my statement perfectly.

WASABI SAUCE

3 tbsp	wasabi mustard	45 mL
3 tbsp	soy sauce	45 mL
3 tbsp	unsalted butter	45 mL
²/₃ cup	black sesame seeds	160 mL
2¹/₂ lbs	fresh ahi tuna steaks	1.2 kg
2–3 tbsp	grapeseed or peanut oil	30–45 mL

GARLIC MASHED POTATOES

3 lb	Yukon gold potatoes, peeled	1.35 kg
3 tbsp	unsalted butter	45 mL
¹/₂ cup	light cream	120 mL
2 heads	roasted garlic (see p. 174)	2 heads
¹/₂ tsp	ground white pepper	2.5 mL
1 tsp	kosher salt	5 mL

SERVES 6

WASABI SAUCE

In a small pot combine the wasabi mustard, soy sauce and butter and simmer until the butter melts. Whisk the mixture until it is smooth and thick. Set aside.

Place the sesame seeds in a shallow dish. Dip both sides of the tuna into the seeds and press so that the seeds adhere to the tuna. Heat a nonstick fry pan to medium high and add the oil. Sear the fish for about 2 minutes on each side, longer if your preference is not rare.

To serve, scoop a portion of the potatoes on the side of the plate. Lean the piece of tuna against the mound of potato and puddle the sauce beside or drizzle it over, whichever you prefer. The taste is a knockout! Mixed vegetables are a perfect side garnish.

GARLIC MASHED POTATOES

Boil the potatoes until tender. Rice or whip the potatoes. Add the butter and cream and mix. Squeeze the cooked garlic pulp into the potatoes and finish with the pepper and kosher salt.

Asian Salmon on a Bed
of Wasabi Mashed Potatoes

The delicious marinade for this recipe is not only quick, it is also easy to prepare. The results are an explosion of Asian flavors that compliment the great texture of Vancouver's wild Pacific salmon. The addition of Wasabi Mashed Potatoes makes it even better—if that's at all possible.

MARINADE

2	shallots, minced	2
2–3	garlic cloves, minced	2–3
2 tbsp	hoisin sauce	30 mL
1 tbsp	oyster sauce	15 mL
1 tbsp	rice vinegar	15 mL
3 tbsp	soy sauce	45 mL
1 tbsp	sesame oil	15 mL
2 lb	fresh wild salmon fillets	900 g

WASABI MASHED POTATOES

1/4 cup	hot water	60 mL
1/4 cup	wasabi	60 mL
3 lb	potatoes, preferably Yukon golds, peeled	1.35 kg
3 tbsp	unsalted butter	45 mL
1/2 cup	light cream	120 mL
to taste	sea salt	
1/2 tsp	ground white pepper	2.5 mL
1/2 cup	chopped fresh cilantro	120 mL

GARNISH

chive stems

SERVES 6

MARINADE

In a small bowl, mix together the shallots, garlic, hoisin sauce, oyster sauce, rice vinegar, soy sauce and sesame oil. Stir well. Spread the marinade over the salmon and refrigerate uncovered for about 2 hours.

Heat an ovenproof fry pan to medium high heat, place the salmon pieces into the pan flesh side down, sear for about 3 minutes, then flip the salmon over. Skin side will now be down. At this point you can continue to cook the salmon in the pan or transfer it to a preheated 375°F (190°C) oven for 10–15 minutes, or until the fish is cooked through.

WASABI MASHED POTATOES

Mix together the water and wasabi. Set aside. Boil the potatoes until tender. While the potatoes are boiling, heat the butter and cream in a small pot and set aside. Drain the potatoes then rice, whip or mash them. Stir in the reserved wasabi and the warmed butter-cream mixture. Season with sea salt and pepper. Add the chopped cilantro.

To serve, place a mound of potatoes in the center of the plate, lay the salmon on top and garnish with chive stems.

CAREN'S ADVICE

Wasabi is a Japanese horseradish. It is grown as a root but more commonly sold in a paste or powdered form. It is pale green in color and packs an intense, fiery, pungent flavor into all it meets. Sushi is a soul mate to wasabi. However, fusion has led it to spread its wings to many cross-cultural foods. Apply where wanted!

Margaret Chisholm's
Porcini-Dusted Sea Bass

Margaret Chisholm is the executive chef at Culinary Capers. She is also a colleague in *The Girls Who Dish* series. We have taught many a class together, with fun and food being equal. Here is one of her specialties.

²/₃ oz	dried porcini mushrooms or powder, *PLANTIN*	20 g
1¹/₂ lbs	Chilean sea bass fillets	675 g
	sea salt	
	freshly ground tellicherry or black pepper	
1	tomato	1
3 tbsp	unsalted butter	45 mL
3 tbsp	red wine	45 mL
1 tbsp	balsamic vinegar	15 mL
1 tbsp	chopped chives	15 mL
	sea salt	
	freshly ground tellicherry or black pepper	

GARNISH

chives

SERVES 4

CAREN'S ADVICE

This fish is simply sublime. It is even more delicious if you coat it with the porcini powder the day before you plan to serve it. This gives the flavor a chance to "bloom." You will need a coffee grinder to grind the dry mushrooms. Clean the grinder before and after using it by grinding a few spoonfuls of uncooked rice for 10 seconds.

Grind the mushrooms to a very fine powder in a coffee grinder. Spread the powder on a small plate. Season the sea bass generously with salt and a little pepper. Dip the sea bass in the powder, coating the fillets evenly. Place the fish on a clean plate, cover and refrigerate for several hours or overnight.

Place enough water to cover the tomato in a pot and bring it to a boil. Cut the core out of the tomato and make a cross in the skin on the bottom. Drop the tomato into the boiling water for 20–30 seconds. Remove with a slotted spoon and place it in a bowl of ice water. When the tomato is cool, the skin will slip right off. Cut in half horizontally. Squeeze gently to remove the seeds. Cut into ¹/₄-inch (.6-cm) dice.

Preheat the oven to 350°F (170°C). Heat a nonstick pan over medium heat. Add 1 tbsp (15 mL) of the butter and when the foam subsides, add the sea bass. Sauté for 1 minute on each side, turning the fish gently. Lift the fish out of the pan and place it on a greased baking sheet. Bake for 8–9 minutes. The fish will be slightly firm and flake a little at the edges when done.

While the fish is cooking, add the remaining butter to the pan. Return to medium heat. Watch very carefully while the butter boils up and begins to brown. When the butter is slightly brown and smells nutty, add the red wine and balsamic vinegar and boil for 2 minutes. Add the tomato and chopped chives. Remove from the heat. Season with salt and pepper.

Spoon some sauce onto individual plates and place the sea bass on top of the sauce. Garnish with a few chives.

Pancetta-Wrapped Snapper
on a Bed of Lentilles du Puy

White fish is generally that, white fish. Without good seasoning or interesting preparations, it reverts back to those days when fish on Friday was the dreaded meal of the week. Try my version of white fish at least once and I guarantee it won't be the last time.

1$\frac{1}{2}$ lbs	fresh snapper, halibut or cod fillets, cut into 6 equal portions	675 g
6 tbsp	pesto sauce, jarred, *INTALIA IN TAVOLA*	90 mL
12 slices	Italian pancetta, thinly sliced	12
$\frac{1}{4}$ cup	extra virgin olive oil	60 mL
2	large shallots, minced	2
1	garlic clove, minced	1
2 tbsp	Dijon mustard	30 mL
$\frac{1}{4}$ cup	sherry vinegar, *CAPIRETE*	60 mL
$\frac{2}{3}$ cup	extra virgin olive oil	160 mL
1 tbsp	preserved lemon, chopped, or 1 tsp lemon zest, grated (5 mL)	15 mL
1 cup	lentilles du Puy (see p. 17) [yields 3 cups (720 mL) cooked]	240 mL
1 tbsp	butter	15 mL
1 cup	silverskin onions, peeled and cut in half	240 mL
1 tsp	sugar	5 mL
1	jar fire-roasted artichokes, drained and sliced (about 8 artichokes)	1
$\frac{1}{4}$ cup	Marsala wine	60 mL
to taste	sea salt	
to taste	freshly ground tellicherry or black pepper	
2–3 tbsp	extra virgin olive oil	30–45 mL

GARNISH

1	fresh lemon, cut in half	1
6 tbsp	each fresh parsley, cilantro and dill, chopped fine	90 mL

SERVES 6

Blot the fish on paper towel. Spread 1 tbsp (15 mL) of pesto on both sides of each fillet. Lay the pancetta on both sides of the fish, using 1 slice for each side. Set aside.

Heat the $\frac{1}{4}$ cup (60 mL) oil in a fry pan, add the shallots and garlic, sauté until just soft, add the mustard and sherry vinegar, slowly whisk in the $\frac{2}{3}$ cup (160 mL) olive oil and the preserved lemon or lemon zest. The mixture will become smooth and thick. Remove from the heat and set aside.

Cook the lentils in plenty of salted boiling water until al dente, about 15–20 minutes. Taste for doneness. Drain well and add the lentils to the reserved sherry/oil mixture.

In a large ovenproof fry pan, heat the butter, add the silverskin onions, and fry for about 5 minutes, then add the sugar to promote browning, shake the pan and toss in the sliced artichokes and the Marsala. Transfer this mixture to the lentils, season with the salt and pepper. In the same pan, heat the 2–3 tbsp (30–45 mL) of olive oil, add the fish and fry for about 2 minutes each side until crispy. Place the pan and the fish in a 400°F (200°C) oven for about 10 minutes, or until the fish is cooked through.

Heat the lentil mixture through, divide evenly onto 6 serving plates, top with a piece of the cooked fish and finish with a squeeze of fresh lemon and a good sprinkle of chopped fresh herbs.

Chicken Filo Packages
with Green Peppercorn Mustard Sauce

Filo seems to provide a nice presentation and crispy finish to almost everything it surrounds. Chicken isn't always the most exciting ingredient but done this way, it has some pizzazz.

3	whole boneless chicken breasts	3
12	stalks fresh asparagus	12
1/4 cup	olive oil	60 mL
3	large shallots, chopped	2
3	garlic cloves, minced	3
1/2 lb	fresh button mushrooms, sliced	225 g
to taste	freshly ground tellicherry or black pepper	
1 lb	filo pastry sheets	455 g
	additional oil for brushing	
6 slices	Black Forest ham	6 slices
6 slices	Swiss or provolone cheese	6 slices
1/3 cup	green peppercorns, brined variety	80 mL
to taste	sea salt	

GREEN PEPPERCORN AND MUSTARD SAUCE

2 oz	butter	60 g
3 tbsp	flour	45 mL
2 cups	chicken stock	480 mL
1	egg yolk	1
2–3 tbsp	heavy cream	30–45 mL
2 tbsp	grainy mustard	30 mL
2–3 tbsp	green peppercorns, brined	30–45 mL
pinch	of pepper	

SERVES 6

Remove all the skin from the chicken and cut into thin strips. Blanch the asparagus in boiling water for about 3 minutes then refresh in cold water. Blot dry and set aside. Heat the 1/4 cup (60 mL) oil in a heavy fry pan, add the shallots and garlic, then toss in the chicken pieces and cook for about 8 minutes. They should almost be cooked through. Add the mushrooms and fry until soft. Season with pepper. Let cool.

Lay the filo out. Brush it with the additional oil, fold in half, brush again with oil. Now lay a small portion of chicken on the filo, a little ham, a few asparagus pieces, a few slices of cheese, and a sprinkle of green peppercorns. Fold the filo into a package, brushing with oil on all sides. Repeat with the rest of the filo. Bake at 375°F (190°C) for about 15 minutes.

Serve with the Green Peppercorn and Mustard Sauce.

GREEN PEPPERCORN AND MUSTARD SAUCE

Melt the butter in a saucier pan, add the flour and cook a few minutes. Whisk in the stock until thickened. Combine the yolk and cream together. Making sure the sauce is not boiling, whisk this into the sauce and simmer. Add the mustard, peppercorns and pepper, adjusting seasoning to taste.

Fennel Roasted Chicken

If you only ever perfect one chicken dish, let this be the one. I have long been a fan of chicken thighs because of their moistness and flavor. Combined with fennel, onion and rosemary, this one-pan dinner is a runaway success for entertaining!

18	large chicken thighs, preferably free range	18
6	large garlic cloves, minced	6
1/2 cup	fresh chopped rosemary	120 mL
1/2 cup	extra virgin olive oil	120 mL
3	large yellow onions, sliced	3
3	large fennel bulbs, sliced, top frond removed and saved	3
3–4 tbsp	extra virgin olive oil	45–60 mL
6 oz	thinly sliced pancetta, chopped	170 mL

GARNISH

fennel fronds or parsley, chopped

SERVES 6

Remove the skin and any excess fat from the chicken. Place in a large bowl. Add the garlic, rosemary and 1/3 cup (80 mL) of the oil. Toss to coat evenly. This can be prepared several hours ahead and refrigerated to marinate the flavors. It is not necessary if you are in a rush.

Preheat the oven to 400°F (200°C). Toss the onions and fennel together, adding the remaining olive oil to coat them lightly. Place the onion and fennel mixture in a 17 x 12 inch (43 x 30 cm) roasting pan. Lay the prepared chicken pieces on top in a single layer.

Bake for 1 hour, turning the chicken at 30 minute intervals. Add the chopped pancetta and cook for 30 minutes more. The chicken should be crispy and brown. Transfer to a serving platter and garnish with chopped fennel fronds if available. If not, chopped parsley will be fine. Wild Mushroom Risotto (see p. 120) is a perfect side dish.

CAREN'S ADVICE

Pancetta is a rolled Italian type of bacon that is not smoked. It is available at all good delis and Italian stores and it comes in spicy or mild. I always choose the spicy variety—because I always like it hot!

The news anchor really can cook. Look out Food Network, he has the talk. Paul Shaw, Tony Parsons and me

Chicken Provençal

with Wild Mushrooms

My inspiration for this dish comes from a small town in Provence called Vaison la Romaine. Our good friend Hervé Poron, who lives there, is our supplier of dried French mushrooms Plantin for which this recipe was created.

There is no substitute for the woodsy, heady flavor derived from the wild dried mushrooms of Provence—once you taste them, you too will be hooked.

¹/₄ cup	each dried morels, boletus and cèpes (or other dried wild mushrooms)	60 mL
5 tbsp	olive oil	75 mL
¹/₄ cup	unbleached all-purpose flour	60 mL
2 lb	chicken thighs, skin removed	900 g
1	large yellow onion, finely diced	1
8	large garlic cloves, peeled	8
2 tbsp	chicken bouillon paste, undiluted, *MAJOR*	30 mL
1	bay leaf	1
to taste	freshly ground tellicherry or black pepper	
1¹/₂ cups	fresh button mushrooms, sliced	360 mL
1 cup	dry white wine	240 mL
¹/₂ cup	heavy cream	120 mL
¹/₄	bunch fresh parsley, finely chopped	¹/₄

SERVES 4–6

Soak the dried wild mushrooms in 2 cups (480 mL) of warm water for about 40 minutes or until reconstituted. Meanwhile, heat 3 tbsp (45 mL) of the olive oil in a cast iron pan and place the flour in a shallow dish.

Dip the chicken into the flour, shaking off the excess, and arrange in the frying pan. Cook, turning the pieces as needed, for about 10 minutes or until the chicken is golden brown on both sides. Transfer to a roasting pan and set aside. Wipe out any excess oil and flour sediment from the frying pan, then heat the remaining 2 tbsp (30 mL) of oil. When hot, add the onion and garlic. Lightly sauté for about 5 minutes or until the onion begins to soften.

Preheat the oven to 350°F (175°C). Drain the mushrooms and, if they seem a little sandy, rinse them again in water. Chop the larger mushrooms and add to the pan of sautéed onions along with the bouillon paste, bay leaf, pepper, fresh mushrooms and wine. Cook for a few minutes, until the bouillon dissolves, and then pour over the chicken.

Cover the roasting pan and bake in the oven 1¹/₂ hours, or until the chicken is cooked through. Remove, transfer to a serving platter, cover and keep warm. Remove the garlic cloves, put them in a small bowl and mash with the back of a spoon. Return garlic to the roaster, place on the stove over medium heat, add the cream and bring sauce to a boil. Taste and adjust the seasonings. Spoon sauce over the chicken and garnish with chopped parsley.

Serve with Cara Nonna's Truffle Pasta.

CAREN'S ADVICE

I like to use an MSG-free bouillion paste called Major.

Chef Boy Slim's Duck

Steve McKinley is the manager of the Gourmet Warehouse and a friend. He has since retired from the professional kitchen but cooks like he never left. He always tells me that the only people who cook duck or order it in restaurants are chefs. He has made this recipe so workable that everyone can cook it, chef or not!

DAY ONE

1/2 cup	celery, finely chopped	120 mL
1 cup	onion, finely chopped	240 mL
1	large head of garlic, chopped coarse, skin on	1
1 tbsp	fleur de sel	15 mL
1 tbsp	rosemary, coarsely chopped	15 mL
2	bay leaves, crumbled	2
1/2	lemon, sliced	1/2
1 1/2 tsp	preserved lemon peel, finely chopped (see p. 23)	7.5 mL
1 tbsp	parsley, chopped	15 mL
	freshly ground black pepper	
1	5 lb. (2.25 kg) fresh or frozen duck, thawed	1

DAY TWO

1/4 cup	shallot, finely chopped	60 mL
1	clove	1
1	2-inch (5-cm) piece of cinnamon stick	1
1/2 cup	sherry	120 mL
1 cup	tomato, chopped	240 mL
2 tbsp	richly flavored olive oil, TENUTA DEL NUMERUNO	30 mL
1/2 cup	pitted small niçoise olives, chopped, ARNAUD	120 mL
1/2 cup	pitted olives, chopped, BELLA DE CERIGNOLA	120 mL
1 tbsp	good quality balsamic vinegar, DEL DUCA	15 mL

SERVES 6-8

DAY ONE

Combine the celery, onion, garlic, fleur de sel, rosemary, bay leaves, lemon, preserved lemon, parsley and pepper to taste in a big bowl, tossing together.

Wash and dry the duck and cut the wing tips off, remove the backbone, and cut into 4 pieces so you have two legs and two breast halves. Trim the excess fat from under the legs and around the breast. Spread half of the vegetable seasoning mixture in a shallow dish. Lay the duck parts—including wing tips and backbone—on top and pack with the remaining vegetables. Cover and marinate in the refrigerator for at least 24 hours or up to 36 hours, if you want.

DAY TWO

Preheat the oven to 300°F (150°C).

Remove all of the duck pieces from the marinade and sauté them over medium heat, carefully browning on all sides. Pour off most of the fat from the fry pan. Add the marinated vegetables, shallots, clove and cinnamon. Sauté until lightly browned.

Place in an earthenware baking dish or casserole dish. Press the browned duck pieces into the mixture. Deglaze the fry pan with the sherry and the tomato and pour over the duck. Cover and bake for 2–3 hours until fork tender.

Remove the duck pieces and place on a baking sheet. Throw away the backbone and wing tips. Strain the rest of the ingredients in the dish through a sieve, pressing down slightly to extract all of the flavor and juices. Remove the fat by skimming.

Transfer this liquid to a saucepan, and begin reducing on high heat until the sauce becomes slightly syrupy. Rub the duck pieces with olive oil and broil them to crisp the skin on both sides. Add the chopped olives and balsamic vinegar to the reduced sauce and serve it on or under the duck, as you prefer.

Roast Turkey

1	turkey about 18 lbs (8.1 kg)	1
to taste	sea salt	
to taste	freshly ground pepper	

GIBLET BROTH

2	onions	2
1	carrot	1
	giblets	
	neck	
	thyme	
1	bay leaf	1
	fresh parsley	
1	recipe Gramma's Turkey Stuffing (see p. 179)	1
1	recipe Perfect Gravy (see p. 181)	1

SERVES 8–10

CAREN'S ADVICE

Stuffing the turkey can be simplified by first lining the cavity of the bird with a cheesecloth. Then, press the prepared stuffing into the lined cavity as normal. Cover the end and roast. To serve the stuffing, simply pull the ends of the cheesecloth to quickly and easily remove the stuffing from the turkey.

PREPARATION

If you purchase a frozen turkey it is imperative that you never thaw it at room temperature. You must let it defrost in the refrigerator or in a sink filled with cold water, immersing the turkey completely. Frozen turkey requires 5 hours per pound (455 g) in the refrigerator to thaw. Alternatively, it takes 1 hour per pound (455 g) to thaw if completely submerged in cold water. Ensure that the water is changed every hour.

Remove the neck and giblets from the inside cavity of the turkey. Rinse the bird and dry out. Season with salt and pepper. Stuff turkey with Gramma's Turkey Stuffing. Cover bird with a tent made out of a supermarket brown paper bag.

GIBLET BROTH

Combine the broth ingredients with 4 cups (960 mL) of water and simmer for 3 hours. Strain and use for gravy.

ROASTING TURKEY

Roast turkey at 450°F (230°C) for 1 hour, then turn down the heat to 400°F (200°C) for the remaining time depending on the size of the bird.

8–12 pound bird (3.6–5.4 kg)	2–3 hours
12–18 pound bird (5.4–8.1 kg)	3–4 hours
18–20 pound bird (8.1–9 kg)	4–4 hours
20–25 pound bird (9–11.25 kg)	4–5 hours

Baste at 30-minute intervals. The turkey is done when the juices run clear. Remove the bag during the last hour of roasting.

Perfection in the kitchen is made extremely easy with the aid of an internal thermometer. It can be digital or dial. Simply insert the probe into the thigh of the bird, ensuring that you do not hit the bone, and the temperature will be registered within a minute. Poultry is safely cooked at 180°F (82°C). The juices should run clear.

Beef Bourguignon

An old French Classic that tastes as good today as it did way back when. You can never tire of a good thing.

¹/₄ lb	diced bacon	114 g
3 lb	round steak, cubed	1.35 kg
	flour for dredging the beef	
20–30	small silverskin onions	20–30
1 tsp	thyme	5 mL
3 tbsp	tomato paste	45 mL
2	garlic cloves, minced	2
2	whole garlic heads, separated and not peeled	2
	bouquet garni (fresh parsley and bay leaf tied together)	
3 cups	red wine	720 mL
1 cup	beef stock	240 mL
10	medium carrots	10
¹/₂ lb	fresh button mushrooms, quartered	225 g
¹/₄ cup	Madeira	60 mL
¹/₄ cup	brandy	60 mL
to taste	ground tellicherry or black pepper	
to taste	sea salt	

GARNISH

parsley, chopped

SERVES 6–8

Fry the bacon in a large sauté pan, remove and set aside. Dredge the beef cubes in the flour (see below) and brown them well in the same pan. Preheat oven to 325°F (165°C). Add the peeled silverskin onions to the pan and brown them well. As soon as the beef and onions are browned, transfer to a large roasting pan. Add the thyme, tomato paste, bouquet garni, wine, stock and both garlics. Cover and place in oven for about 1¹/₂ hours or until the beef is tender.

Peel and coarsely chop the carrots and add them to the roasting pan. Cook for a further 25 minutes then add the mushrooms to the roasting pan for the last 15 minutes of cooking.

When the meat is cooked and tender throughout, stir in the Madeira and brandy. Season with ground pepper and sea salt. If you find the sauce too thin, thicken it with 2–3 tablespoons (30–45mL) of beurre manie (see below). Whisk it into the sauce a tablespoon at a time.

Ladle the beef over buttered noodles or serve it alongside roasted potatoes. A generous sprinkle of chopped parsley gives a simple garnish.

CAREN'S ADVICE
Beurre manie is a French term, meaning kneaded butter. Made using equal portions of butter and flour (i.e. 3 tbsp/45 mL butter mixed with 3 tbsp/ 45 mL flour), it is used to thicken sauces. When whisked in it provides a lump-free sauce.

DREDGING BEEF CUBES
Place the flour in a plastic produce bag, drop the beef cubes into the flour bag, shake to coat. When you finish, simply throw the bag away.

Rob Feenie's Braised Short Ribs
and Sauce Bordelaise

Lumière is the very bright light in Vancouver's restaurant scene. The one holding the light bulb is none other than Rob Feenie, a most creative chef. His short ribs demand at the very minimum a double order. What a break, you can now make triple orders in the privacy of your own kitchen. The only thing missing might be Rob's beautiful oversized white dishes that make delicious food spectacular.

BRAISED SHORT RIBS

2 lb	beef short ribs, cut 1³/₄ inches (4 cm) thick	900 g
to taste	salt	
to taste	freshly ground white pepper	
2 tbsp	vegetable oil	30 mL
3	shallots, finely chopped	3
6	garlic cloves, crushed	6
12	whole black peppercorns	12
¹/₂ cup	ruby port	120 mL
1 cup	dry red wine	240 mL
2–3 cups	veal or beef stock	480–720 mL
2	bay leaves	2
8	sprigs thyme	8

SAUCE BORDELAISE

1 cup	red wine	240 mL
¹/₃ cup	sliced shallots	75 mL
2	sprigs thyme	2
1	bay leaf	1
1 tbsp	garlic	15 mL

SERVES 4

BRAISED SHORT RIBS

Preheat oven to 350°F (175°C).

Trim excess fat from short ribs. Sprinkle both sides of ribs with salt and freshly ground white pepper.

In a Dutch oven, heat oil over medium-high heat. Add ribs and brown on all sides for 5–7 minutes. Transfer ribs to plate; set aside. Remove all but 1 tbsp (15 mL) fat from pan.

Reduce heat to medium and add shallots and garlic to Dutch oven. Cook, covered for 2 minutes. Add port and wine, stirring to deglaze bottom of pan. Add stock, bay leaves, thyme, peppercorns and browned ribs, and bring to a boil. Transfer pan to oven for 4–5 hours, or until meat is falling off the bone, turning meat occasionally. Remove meat from bones and keep warm.

Strain cooking liquid into a large saucepan. Bring to a simmer and cook for 10–12 minutes or until reduced by half. You should have about 1³/₄ cups (420 mL). Reserve liquid for sauce.

Taste and adjust seasoning.

SAUCE BORDELAISE

In a medium pan bring the wine, shallots, thyme, bay leaf and garlic to a simmer until almost all the liquid has evaporated. Add the reduce braising liquid and simmer for a further 10–15 minutes, or until the stock is reduced to a sauce consistency, about ³/₄ cup (180 mL). Strain the sauce through a fine-mesh strainer into a saucepan. The sauce can be refrigerated for up to 3 days.

Ribs to Fight For!

Grilling seems to be synonymous with guys, a kind of testosterone-building thing that goes on between man and his grill. With their Fred Flintstone image, ribs are either very good or very bad. The secret of good ribs lies in a long simmer to tenderize them. My mother is the master of ribs in our house. She maintains a watch over the large pot of simmering ribs then proclaims them ready to grill.

8–10	racks baby back ribs (allow about 6–8 ribs per person)	8–10
1	yellow onion, cut into quarters	1
1	large carrot, cut into chunks	1
1	bay leaf	1
8–10	whole peppercorns	8–10
1	celery stalk, cut into chunks	1
1 tsp	sea salt	5 mL
8 oz	your favorite marinade or barbecue sauce, *TEQUILA-LIME*™	227 mL

SERVES 6–8

Place the ribs, onion, carrot, bay leaf, peppercorns, celery and salt in a large pot. Cover with water and bring to a boil. Reduce the heat and let the ribs simmer for about 60 minutes—they will be pliable when ready. Remove the ribs and discard the ingredients left in the pot.

Place the ribs on a baking tray and slather them generously with the barbecue sauce. Grill over medium high heat, brushing the ribs with additional sauce as required. Turn and brush until the ribs are golden and almost falling from the bone. Transfer to a serving platter and chow down!

José Valagao, me and Hervé Martin

Foie Gras-Stuffed Beef Tenderloin

What a decadent way to serve beef, stuffed with foie gras! I like to use Georges Bruck foie gras, a great product from France. It is purchased tinned and can be served on its own, with bread, or in this case, stuffed into the center of beef tenderloin. Anyway you slice it, this dish is one all guests will enjoy.

2 lb	whole beef tenderloin	900 g
7 oz	tinned pâté de foie gras, well chilled, *GEORGES BRUCK*	200 g
	extra virgin olive oil	
¼ cup	cracked Italian pepper	60 mL
1	recipe Quick Classic Demi-Glaze (see p. 177)	1

SERVES 6

Butterfly the beef (open it out flat) and lightly pound it to ensure that it is of even thickness. Lay the foie gras down the center of the meat. Roll the meat up to encircle the foie gras. Tie with kitchen string about every 2 inches (5 cm).

Rub with olive oil and press the pepper onto the beef to form a crust. Heat your barbecue to high and grill the tenderloin until cooked to your required doneness.

An internal temperature of 140°F (60°C) will be rare.

Let the meat rest for at least 10–15 minutes before slicing. Serve with the demi-glaze.

Vincent Heusch (Frenchie), me, Valerie Schlaufmann and José Valagao

Osso Buco

Meaty veal shanks are slow cooked in this flavorful, classic recipe. Regardless of your cooking ability, this dish is so easy and foolproof, it will bring you accolades like never before. What are you waiting for?

5 tbsp	olive oil	75 mL
4 tbsp	butter	60 mL
6	veal shanks, cut from the hind shank	6
1/2 cup	unbleached all-purpose flour	120 mL
2	large onions, diced	2
2	medium carrots, peeled and finely diced	2
1	celery stalk, finely diced	1
3	large garlic cloves, minced	3
1/2	bunch fresh parsley, chopped	1/2
2 cups	canned Roma tomatoes, chopped	480 mL
2	sprigs fresh sage	2
2	bay leaves	2
1 cup	beef stock	240 mL
1 cup	dry white wine	240 mL
to taste	sea salt	
to taste	freshly ground tellicherry or black pepper	
2–3 tbsp	preserved lemon, chopped (see p. 23)	30–45 mL

GARNISH

parsley, chopped

SERVES 6

Heat 2 tbsp (30 mL) each of the oil and butter in a heavy cast iron pan. Dip the veal shanks into the flour, shaking off the excess, and sear them in the hot pan for 4–6 minutes until golden brown on both sides. Remove and set aside.

In the same pan, heat the remaining 3 tbsp (45 mL) oil and 2 tbsp (30 mL) butter. When hot, add the onions, carrots, celery, garlic and parsley. Sauté for 10 minutes until soft. Add the tomatoes, sage, bay leaves, stock, wine, salt and pepper. Cook over medium heat for about 15 minutes so that the flavors marry.

Preheat the oven to 350°F (175°C). Spoon a small portion of the vegetable mixture on the bottom of a baking pan. Arrange the veal shanks on top in a single layer. Top with the remaining vegetables. Cover the pan with foil and bake for 2–3 hours until the meat almost falls from the bone. Check the pan from time to time to ensure that it doesn't dry out. Add a little more wine if required.

To serve, transfer the shanks to a platter and stir the preserved lemon into the pan juices. Ladle over the shanks and serve. Garnish with the parsley. I love it with risotto.

Stuffed Pork Tenderloin
with Stilton Port Sauce

This is probably as close to its 15 minutes of fame that pork will ever get. Usually it's delegated down the food line as not the meat of choice. With the help of this recipe's flavor combinations, pork can now soar to new heights. My good friend, awesome broadcaster and fellow food lover Bill Good has championed this recipe to its deserved accolades. It was one of the very first recipes that we broadcasted together on his radio show on CKNW/98 years ago. Its popularity has not waned, I still get weekly requests. Now it's your turn to turn up the heat for pork!

3 lb	pork tenderloin	1.35 kg
3^1/2 oz	prosciutto di Parma	100 g
3^1/2 oz	Asiago cheese	100 g
3 tbsp	extra virgin olive oil	45 mL
3	shallots, finely minced	3
1	large garlic clove, minced	1

SAUCE

^{1}/2 cup	red wine	120 mL
2 cups	beef stock	480 mL
2 tbsp	infused or plain balsamic vinegar	30 mL
^{1}/2 cup	heavy cream	120 mL
5 oz	English Stilton blue cheese, Roquefort or Gorgonzola	160 mL
^{1}/3 cup	port wine	80 mL
2 tbsp	green peppercorns in brine, drained	30 mL
to taste	sea salt	
to taste	freshly ground tellicherry or black pepper	

SERVES 6–8

TO PREPARE THE PORK

Cut the pork loin down the center and butterfly (open it out flat). If the flesh is uneven pound it out until the meat is even. Lay the prosciutto and Asiago down the middle of the loin. Roll the pork up and tie it at intervals so that it will not open during cooking. You can prepare the pork to this point and refrigerate until serving time.

Preheat the oven to 400°F (200°C). Heat a sauté pan to medium high heat, add the oil, shallots and garlic to the pan. Sauté for about 3 minutes until soft. Add the tenderloin to the pan and sear on all sides. Transfer the pork to a baking sheet and roast in the oven for 20 minutes. While the pork is roasting, prepare the sauce.

SAUCE

In the same pan as you seared the pork, pour in the wine, scraping up the fried bits from the bottom of the pan. Add the stock and bring to a boil. Continue to boil until the liquid is reduced by half. Add the balsamic vinegar, continuing to simmer. Pour in the heavy cream, keep the heat on medium and continue to cook for a further 5 minutes. Add the Stilton and port along with the peppercorns.

Keep the heat on low until the sauce is thick enough to coat the back of a spoon. Season with sea salt and pepper. To serve, puddle the sauce in the center of the plate, arrange the sliced pork over top and garnish with your choice of vegetables around the outside of the plate.

Leg of Lamb

Grainy mustard and lamb's favorite herb, rosemary, make this an easy yet spectacular main course.

4–5 lb	leg of lamb	1.8–2.25 kg
1/3 cup	grainy mustard	80 mL
2	garlic cloves, minced	2
2 tsp	herbes de Provence	10 mL
3 tbsp	fresh rosemary, chopped	45 mL
to taste	Italian pepper, cracked	
1/3 cup	extra virgin olive oil	80 mL
6	garlic cloves, peeled and cut in half	6

DEMI-GLAZE

2	heads roasted garlic (see p. 174)	2
	red wine for deglazing the pan	
1 cup	beef stock	240 mL
5–6	shiitake mushrooms, sliced	5–6

SERVES 8–10

Trim all excess fat from the lamb and discard. Mix the mustard, garlic, herbs, pepper and oil together. Set aside.

Using a small knife, make a slit about 1-inch (2.5-cm) down into the flesh of the leg. Insert the garlic halves, trying to keep the insertions evenly spaced.

Rub the leg with the mustard mixture and place in a roasting pan. Sear the meat at 450°F (230°C) for 10–15 minutes. Reduce the temperature to 350°F (180°C). For rare meat, cook for 10 minutes per pound (455 g), including searing time. For medium meat, 12–15 minutes per pound (455 g) and for well done, 20 minutes per pound (455 g).

DEMI-GLAZE

When the lamb is done, place it on a carving board. Remove any excess grease from the roaster. Place the roaster on the element at medium heat. Add the red wine and stock to deglaze the pan. Reduce by about half. Add the shiitake mushrooms and cook about 3 minutes. Toss in the roasted garlic, adjust the seasonings and spoon over lamb slices.

Mustard and Herb-Crusted Lamb Loins

Lamb loins are those wonderful no-fat, no-bones, no-work cuts of meat. Slathered with a herb mustard crust, this dish is a no-brainer.

1/3 cup	Dijon mustard	75 mL
4	garlic cloves, minced	4
3 tbsp	extra virgin olive oil	45 mL
2 tbsp	fresh thyme, finely chopped	30 mL
2 tbsp	fresh basil, finely chopped	30 mL
2 tbsp	fresh rosemary, finely chopped	30 mL
1 tbsp	fresh sage, finely chopped	15 mL
1 1/2 tsp	sea salt	7.5 mL
1 tbsp	freshly cracked black pepper	15 mL
1 1/2 lb	lamb loins	750 g

SERVES 6

In a medium bowl, combine the Dijon mustard, garlic and oil. Stir all the herbs into the mustard mixture. Stir in the sea salt and pepper.

Rub the garlic and herb mixture over both sides of the loins. Heat your barbecue or grill to high, and grill each side for about 3–4 minutes (for medium-rare). Turn the meat only once so that it doesn't dry out.

Serve immediately.

Big smiles as the conclusion of Flora Springs Wine Auction dinner nears. Winery intern, me, Diane Lawrence, Bob Lawrence, Winery intern (Flora Springs, California)

Karen Barnaby's Lamb Shanks
with Red Split Lentils

Karen Barnaby, friend, author and executive chef at the Fish House in Vancouver, has generously shared one of her favorite dishes. Karen says black cardamom and curry leaves can be found in Indian food stores. If they are unavailable, just add 2 more green cardamom pods.

1¹/₂ cups	red split lentils	360 mL
4 cups	water	950 mL
¹/₂ tsp	turmeric	2.5 mL
4 tbsp	vegetable oil	60 mL
4	whole green cardamom pods	4
2	whole black cardamom pods	2
1¹/₂-inch	cinnamon stick	3.75-cm
1	medium onion, cut into thin half moons	1
6	meaty lamb shanks	6
1 tsp	fresh ginger, finely grated	5 mL
1 tsp	garlic, finely chopped	5 mL
¹/₂ tsp	cayenne pepper	2.5 mL
to taste	sea salt	

LENTIL SEASONING

2 tbsp	tamarind concentrate	30 mL
¹/₂ tsp	cayenne pepper	2.5 mL
to taste	sea salt	

SAUCE

2 tbsp	clarified butter or vegetable oil	30 mL
1 tsp	cumin seeds	5 mL
1–2	dried hot chilies	1–2
8–10	fresh curry leaves (optional)	8–10
2	garlic cloves, peeled and cut in half lengthwise	2

SERVES 4–6

Pick over the lentils for stones and wash in several changes of cold water. Add the lentils and water to a heavy pot. Bring to a boil, skim off the foam and add the turmeric. Reduce to a bare simmer, partially covered with a lid. Cook for 1 hour or until the lentils are soft.

Preheat the oven to 300°F (150°C). While the lentils are cooking, heat the 4 tbsp (60 mL) of vegetable oil in a large ovenproof pot over medium heat. Add the cardamom and cinnamon and cook until the cardamom darkens. Add the onion and fry until lightly browned. Add the shanks and stir until they brown a little. Add the ginger, garlic and ¹/₂ tsp (2.5 mL) cayenne and season with salt. Add water to barely cover and bring to a simmer. Cover and transfer to the oven and cook for 2–2¹/₂ hours until the meat is tender, adding more water if needed to keep the level up to the original.

LENTIL SEASONING

Add the tamarind and remaining ¹/₂ tsp (2.5 mL) cayenne to the lentils and season with salt. When the meat is tender, add the lentils and simmer for 15 minutes.

SAUCE

Before serving, heat the 2 tbsp (30 mL) of clarified butter or vegetable oil over medium heat. Add the cumin seeds. When they darken, add the chilies and curry leaves, if using. When the chilies darken, add the garlic. As soon as the garlic turns light brown, pour the entire mixture over the pot of lamb and lentils. Serve immediately.

condiments, sauces & beverages

Roasted Garlic

whole bulbs of garlic

olive oil

foil for roasting

SERVES 6–8

To roast garlic, preheat the oven to 325°F (165°C). Make a straight cut, about ¹/₄ inch (.6 cm) deep, across the stem end of the garlic bulb, exposing the cloves. Rub the bulb with olive oil and pour a little oil in the center of a piece of foil. Place the garlic cut side down on the foil. Wrap the foil around the bulb. Roast for 45–60 minutes. Don't be tempted to speed the process by raising the oven temperature—it will often result in bitter garlic. Different types of garlic from different growing regions take varying amounts of time, but it generally takes close to an hour for the sugar in the garlic to develop, giving it the characteristic mellow flavor. When it's done, it should be caramel-colored and soft in texture. If not, return it to the oven for another 15 minutes. Let the garlic cool in the foil. Remove the cloves with a knife tip or squeeze them out of the papery husks.

Fig, Onion Confit

8	medium-sized white onions	8
4 tbsp	extra virgin olive oil	60 mL
¹/₄ cup	balsamic vinegar	60 mL
¹/₄ cup	port wine	60 mL
²/₃ cup	brown sugar	160 mL
1 cup	Black Mission or Calimyrna figs, quartered	240 mL
to taste	freshly ground tellicherry or black pepper	

MAKES 3–4 CUPS (720 ML–1 L)

Fig, Onion Confit is quite simply a fabulous thick savory mixture of onions, port and figs. Dollop this ultra-yummy jam on cheese, chicken, burgers, beef, pork or simply eat it all on its own.

Slice the onions as thinly as possible. Heat the oil in a large sauté pan, add the onions and sauté on medium heat for about 15–20 minutes. Stir only occasionally. If the onions begin to scorch or stick put the lid on to create some moisture.

When the onions are a dark caramel brown, after about 20 minutes or so, add the balsamic vinegar, port, sugar and figs. Cook for an additional 15 minutes, or until the mixture is thick like a marmalade. Adjust the seasonings with pepper.

Roasted Chestnuts and Caramelized Onions

This is my favorite fall condiment. Chestnuts produce an image of Europe, where every block has wagons fitted with glowing charcoal, roasting fragrant whole chestnuts in huge warped but perfectly seasoned pans. The liberal addition of coarse sea salt makes these mahogany nuggets all the better. At home, I roast them in the oven. It's not quite like being on the streets of Paris or Florence, but one can imagine!

1 lb	Italian chestnuts	455 g
1/2 lb	silverskin onions or small shallots	225 g
3 tbsp	butter	45 mL
2 tsp	sugar	10 mL
1/2 cup	white wine	120 mL
to taste	sea salt	
to taste	cracked tellicherry pepper or black pepper	

SERVES 6–8

With a sharp knife, make a cross on the flat side of each chestnut. Place all the chestnuts on a cookie sheet and bake them for about 1 hour at 350°F (175°C). Shake the pan occasionally during baking, so they toast evenly.

Meanwhile bring a large pot of water to the boil, drop the onions in the water and let them blanch for about 5 minutes. Remove and place in cold water at once. This will make the peeling much easier.

Remove the chestnuts from the oven and peel immediately. If you wait until the chestnuts are cool, the inside skin will adhere to the nut and make it impossible to peel. Use gloves if necessary.

Heat the butter in a cast iron pan. Add the peeled onions and let them sauté for about 10 minutes. Sprinkle in the sugar and shake the pan around to promote the caramelization or browning. Cut the chestnuts into quarters and toss them into the pan. Let them heat through for about 5 minutes. Pour in the wine and let it reduce to almost nothing. Add seasoning to taste.

Serve warm or at room temperature. Great with roast turkey or any grilled meats.

CAREN'S ADVICE

When purchasing chestnuts, always squeeze them. They should be full, meaning no hollow parts. If you squeeze them and the shell buckles, this indicates the chestnut is old and has shrunk away from the shell. Try another vendor and always buy the Italian variety. They are the most flavorful nuts.

Mango Chutney

For all you purists who like quality, here is a chutney that is relatively uncomplicated and quick to prepare. I like to serve it with curry or spread over a chicken sandwich. Add half a small chopped chili to the pot if spice is your life!

¹/₄ cup	brown sugar	60 mL
¹/₄ cup	white vinegar	60 mL
¹/₃ cup	raisins	80 mL
4	whole cloves	4
¹/₂ tsp	fresh nutmeg, grated	2.5 mL
¹/₂ tsp	cinnamon	2.5 mL
	pinch of salt	
1	small onion, finely chopped	1
2 cups	mango, coarsely chopped	480 mL
2 tbsp	water	30 mL
2 tbsp	fresh lime juice	30 mL

MAKES 1 CUP (240 ML)

In a non-reactive pan, combine the sugar, vinegar, raisins, cloves, nutmeg, cinnamon, salt and onion. Bring the mixture to a boil, then reduce to a slow simmer for about 10 minutes. Add the mango and 2 tbsp (30 mL) water, then simmer until thick. Stir often.

Remove from heat and stir in the lime juice. Cool to room temperature. Will store up to one week in the refrigerator.

Balsamic Syrup

Tradizionale balsamic is one of those ultimately unaffordable condiments that we only read about. The chef's secret is to take an inexpensive, commercial, non-aged balsamic and to boil it down to a fraction of its original volume. I urge you to make this and keep it on hand for whenever a sauce needs some oomph or a dish requires a flavorful dab of garnish.

1 (17 oz)	bottle balsamic vinegar, *DEL DUCA*	1 (500 mL)

MAKES ¹/₂ CUP (120 ML)

Place the vinegar in a stainless steel pot and boil until reduced to ¹/₂ cup (120 mL). Cool and refrigerate until needed.

Quick Classic Demi-Glaze

Remember that fabulous sauce you couldn't get enough of but the restaurant refused to disclose its secret? Usually, without a brigade of sauciers, home cooks are reduced to tasty but basic gravy! Here is a sauce that will have your guests dancing on table tops for more.

4 tbsp	butter	60 mL
2	medium onions, diced	2
2	medium carrots, chopped	2
3	large sprigs fresh parsley	3
3	sprigs fresh thyme	3
2 tbsp	sugar	30 mL
3 tbsp	unbleached flour	45 mL
3 cups	beef stock	720 mL
1 tbsp	tomato paste	15 mL
1	bay leaf	1
2 tbsp	cognac or brandy	30 mL
2 tbsp	Madeira or Marsala	30 mL
to taste	sea salt	
to taste	freshly ground tellicherry or black pepper	

MAKES 3 CUPS (720 ML)

Melt the butter in a 3 qt (3.4 L) pot. Add the onions, carrots, parsley and thyme and sauté until vegetables are very dark and caramelized—about 30 minutes. During the last 10 minutes of cooking add the sugar to promote deeper color.

Stir in the flour and cook on low for 2–3 minutes. Whisk in the stock, tomato paste and the bay leaf. Let the sauce simmer for about 15 minutes with the lid off, stirring occasionally.

Strain the sauce through a fine mesh sieve, pushing very hard on the vegetables so that you extract all the flavor. Return the sauce to the pot and add the cognac or brandy and Madeira or Marsala.

Adjust the seasonings to taste. Serve this sauce with any grilled Madeira or meat dish.

OPTIONS
Add 1/2 cup (120 mL) baby morel mushrooms or 1/3 cup (75 mL) brined green or pink peppercorns for a different flavor.

Ruth Grierson, Clara McSherry and Doreen Corday

Curry Sauce

Curry has long been a favorite of mine. This sauce is quick and easy, and can be served over any vegetable, meat or rice dish. The secret is to find a superb curry powder. Once you find the blend you like, it's complete. My favorite is Monsoon Coast.

3–4 tbsp	unsalted butter	45–60 mL
2 cups	Spanish onion, finely diced	480 mL
2	garlic cloves, minced	2
1 tsp	hot pepper, chopped (optional)	5 mL
2 tbsp	fresh ginger, minced	30 mL
3–4 tbsp	curry powder, *MONSOON COAST*	45–60 mL
1 (14 oz)	can of coconut milk	1 (400 g)
1/2	lemon, juice of	1/2
4 tbsp	chutney, *MAJOR GREY*	60 mL
1 tsp	undiluted chicken paste or cube, *MAJOR*	5 mL
to taste	sea salt	

MAKES 2 CUPS (480 ML)

Heat the butter in a medium-sized sauce pan, add the onion, garlic, hot pepper if using and ginger. Cook until the onion is soft but not browned. Sprinkle in the curry powder and stir for 1–2 minutes. Whisk in the coconut milk until it is smooth. Add the lemon juice, chutney and chicken paste. Whisk until combined. Simmer for about 15 minutes to thicken and intensify the flavors. Add sea salt to taste. Chill any leftovers for up to 4 days.

Béchamel Sauce

One of the very basics of classic French cuisine, béchamel, or white sauce as we know it, is the very foundation of many other sauces. By adding cheese, it becomes a Mornay. By substituting chicken stock for milk, it becomes velouté.

3 tbsp	unsalted butter	45 mL
1/4 cup	unbleached all-purpose flour	60 mL
2 cups	whole milk	480 mL
1/2 tsp	sea salt	2.5 mL
pinch	ground white pepper	
pinch	fresh ground nutmeg	

MAKES 2 CUPS (480 ML)

Melt the butter in a saucepan. Add the flour and stir for 3 minutes on low heat. This step is vital as it cooks the flour so the sauce will not have a floury taste.

Add the milk a little at a time, whisking until thick and smooth. Remove from the heat. Add the salt, pepper and nutmeg.

Avocado Papaya Salsa

If guacamole excites you, hold yourself back. This is as good as it gets—for avocados that is!

2	ripe avocados, peeled and coarsely chopped	2
1	ripe papaya, peeled, seeded and coarsely chopped	1
2	garlic cloves, minced	2
$^2/_3$ cup	purple onion, finely chopped	160 mL
3	large Roma tomatoes, diced	3
$^1/_2$	fresh lemon, juice of	$^1/_2$
to taste	piri piri (see p. 54) or other hot sauce	
to taste	sea salt	
to taste	freshly ground tellicherry or black pepper	
1 tsp	Worcestershire sauce	5 mL

MAKES 3 CUPS (720 ML)

Place the avocados and papaya in a glass bowl. Add the garlic, onion, tomatoes, lemon juice, hot sauce and seasoning. Mix well to combine but do not overmix.

Gramma's Turkey Stuffing

Gramma's turkey stuffing is just that—stuffing with Gramma's touch. Comforting, tasty and above all simple, it is usually the focus of the festive meal. Personalize it to suit your tastes by adding chestnuts, pecans or sausage.

3 tbsp	butter	45 mL
4	stalks celery, finely diced	4
$^1/_2$	large onion, finely diced	$^1/_2$
4 cups	coarse dry breadcrumbs	950 mL
1 tsp	poultry seasoning	5 mL
2 cups	chicken stock	480 mL
to taste	sea salt	
to taste	freshly ground tellicherry or black pepper	

MAKES 4 HEAPING CUPS (1 L)

Melt the butter in a medium skillet, add the celery and onion. Sauté until soft, but not brown. Transfer to a large bowl and add the breadcrumbs. Sprinkle in the poultry seasoning. Toss well with your hands to evenly distribute the ingredients. Gradually pour in the chicken stock, a little at a time, just enough to moisten the breadcrumbs. You may not need all the stock. Finish by seasoning with sea salt and fresh tellicherry pepper.

Crème Fraîche

Crème fraîche is one of those magical ingredients from the masters of classic French cuisine. Unlike the intimidating sauces that hail from the likes of Escoffier and Bocusé, crème fraîche is something home cooks can master just by reading. Go ahead, you too can conquer the French kitchen—well for this recipe at least!

1 cup	whipping cream	240 mL
4 tbsp	sour cream or buttermilk	60 mL

MAKES 1 CUP (240 ML)

Combine the whipping cream and sour cream together in a glass jar. Let the mixture sit overnight at room temperature. Once thick, refrigerate. The crème fraîche will keep for up to one week in the refrigerator.

CAREN'S ADVICE

Crème fraîche is the wonder sauce of the kitchen, providing that extra boost at the last minute. Use it to spoon over fruit cobblers, add a dollop to liven up weak dressings and, of course, use as the crowning glory on caviar or to sit alongside smoked salmon.

Parmesan and Black Pepper Dressing

If salad dressing could become habitual, then this is certainly a contender. Let's face it, who doesn't like freshly grated Parmesan or pepper?

1 cup	buttermilk	240 mL
1/2 cup	mayonnaise, *HELLMAN'S*	120 mL
1/2 cup	Parmesan cheese, freshly grated	120 mL
1	garlic clove, minced	1
1	shallot, minced	1
1 tsp	freshly ground black pepper	5 mL
to taste	sea salt	

MAKES 1 1/2 CUPS (360 ML)

Whisk all the ingredients together until the dressing is smooth and creamy. Chill for at least 1 hour before serving.

Perfect Gravy

A classic term of the 1950s and 1960s, gravy was always served for company, alongside roast beef, chicken, turkey, even pot roast. Today its great taste and appeal remain the same, only the name has changed. The food police of the 1980s elevated gravy's status to sauce. However, in our house, whenever we enjoy a turkey dinner, it is "please pass the gravy." Sauce is reserved for other menus. This gravy is based on turkey.

²/₃ cup	unbleached all-purpose flour	160 mL
3–4 cups	water	720–960 mL
to taste	sea salt	
to taste	freshly ground tellicherry or black pepper	

MAKES 3–4 CUPS (720–960 ML)

Remove the turkey from the roasting pan. Place the pan on the stove top to keep hot. Remove any large bits and pieces of the turkey that may have fallen off during roasting. Turn the heat to low. Sprinkle the flour over the pan. Using a large whisk, stir the flour into the pan juices, whisking vigorously.

Once you've been whisking for about 2 minutes and the flavor has been absorbed, slowly pour in the water about 1 cup (240 mL) at a time, whisking constantly.

Continue to add the water until the gravy meets your desired consistency. The more liquid you add, the thinner the gravy will be. Season with sea salt and pepper.

OPTIONS

If you are serving potatoes with this meal, save the cooking water from the potatoes to use in place of plain water.

A nice addition is ¹/₄ cup (60 mL) of red or white wine.

CAREN'S ADVICE FOR PERFECT GRAVY
Never use cooked vegetable water. The result is often bitter, especially cauliflower water. Using potato water is the *only* exception.

Glenys's Chipotle Bourbon
Cranberry Sauce

I thought for a long while that I had the line on the best cranberry sauce ever! That was until my colleague and friend, Glenys Morgan, prepared her version. A turkey should not emerge from the oven, nor a sandwich be prepared, until Glenys's cranberry sauce is at the ready. Needless to say my cranberry recipe has not only hit the back burner, but has been fully retired with her condiment in its stead. Thanks, Glenys!

1 (12 oz)	pkg cranberries, fresh or frozen	1 (340 g)
2 cups	apple juice or cider	480 mL
2	cinnamon sticks	2
4–6	clusters star anise (available from Asian food stores)	4–6
1 cup	dark brown sugar	240 mL
2–3	chipotle chilies in adobo sauce	2–3
1/4 cup	bourbon	60 mL
2	limes, juice of	2

MAKES 1 1/4 CUPS (300 ML)

In a non-reactive saucepan, combine the cranberries, juice or cider, cinnamon sticks and star anise clusters. To manage how sweet the sauce will be, begin with $1/2$ cup (120 mL) sugar. The rest may be added later to taste. Bring the berries to a boil, then reduce the heat to medium-low. The cranberries will cook completely in 20–30 minutes, bursting and turning the sauce deep red. In the last few minutes of cooking, taste for sweetness and stir in more sugar as desired. Remove from the heat and allow to cool slightly.

To make mincing the chilis easier, cut them on foil or parchment. After scraping them into the pot, discard the paper. For a milder smoky flavor, omit the chipotles and spoon some of the adobo sauce into the cranberries. Add the bourbon and lime juice. The high natural pectin in cranberries keeps the sauce for months in the refrigerator.

Roquefort Dressing to Die For!

Roquefort dressing always brings back memories of wait staff reciting "Would you prefer French, Thousand Island or Italian dressing with your salad? Oh, Roquefort is 50 cents extra." Now that I have truly dated myself with old memories, here is a Roquefort dressing worth remembering.

1	garlic clove, minced	1
1 tbsp	Dijon mustard	15 mL
1/2 cup	sour cream	120 mL
1/2 cup	mayonnaise, *HELLMAN'S*	120 mL
1 tsp	Worcestershire sauce	5 mL
1/2 lb	French Roquefort, crumbled	225 g
to taste	sea salt	
to taste	freshly ground tellicherry or black pepper	
1/4 cup	port or sweet sherry	60 mL
1	head iceberg lettuce	1
36	small grape or cherry tomatoes	36

SERVES 6

Place the minced garlic in a bowl with the mustard, sour cream and mayonnaise. Stir well to combine the ingredients. Add the Worcestershire sauce and crumbled cheese and stir. Season with the sea salt and pepper. Slowly pour in the port or sherry, stirring as you pour, until the desired consistency is reached. Pour the dressing over crisp wedges of iceberg, garnished with those lovely little grape or cherry tomatoes.

Me and Julia Child

Saffron Sauce

Saffron sauce is one of those magical tastes you never forget. It is a true reflection of the labor and cost involved in just one gram of this jewel of a spice. Use on grilled salmon, prawns, scallops or crab. It makes a terrific pasta sauce served over top of black linguine.

1¼ cups	fish or chicken stock	300 mL
1	large shallot, finely chopped	1
2 tsp	fresh ginger, chopped	10 mL
1	garlic clove, chopped	1
½ cup	white wine	120 mL
1	sprig of fresh thyme	1
1½ cups	heavy cream	360 mL
1 tsp	saffron threads, pounded	5 mL
½	fresh lemon, juiced	½

MAKES 1½ CUPS (360 ML)

Combine the stock, shallot, ginger, garlic, wine and thyme. Bring to a boil and reduce by half.

Pour through a fine mesh strainer, discard the bits and return the liquid to the pot. Add the cream and saffron. Simmer until thick enough to coat the back of a spoon. Season to taste and finish with a squeeze of fresh lemon juice.

Publisher and author seal the deal: Robert McCullough and me.

Wild Mushroom Sauce

Wild mushrooms have long been a passion of the French. In North America, we have just recently come to embrace the exotic flavors that these intense morsels possess. I am a big fan of the dried variety; however, when the season is upon us for the fresh, use them in abundance. Here is my version of a spectacular mushroom sauce that can be used for pasta, an accent to grilled poultry and meats or simply smeared on a crusty baguette.

3	large shallots, minced	3
1	large garlic clove, minced	1
3 tbsp	unsalted butter or extra virgin olive oil	45 mL
2 tbsp	balsamic vinegar	30 mL
1 cup	shiitake mushrooms, sliced	240 mL
1 cup	fresh chanterelle mushrooms, sliced	240 mL
1 cup	fresh portobello mushrooms, sliced	240 mL
1/2 cup	chicken or beef stock	120 mL
1/2 cup	Marsala wine or sweet sherry	120 mL
1 tbsp	fresh thyme, chopped	15 mL
1/3 cup	heavy cream	80 mL
to taste	sea salt	
to taste	freshly ground tellicherry or black pepper	

SERVES 6–10

Sauté the shallots and garlic in the butter or oil. Take care to only soften, not brown them. Add the balsamic vinegar to the pan along with the sliced mushrooms. Sauté for about 5 minutes. Add the stock and cover for about 2 minutes. Remove the lid and cook until the mushrooms begin to reduce.

Add the Marsala or sherry and fresh thyme to the pan, continuing to simmer until the liquid is reduced by half.

Pour in the cream, stirring to combine. Keep the heat on low until the sauce is thick. Adjust the seasoning with sea salt and freshly ground pepper.

Perfect Caramel Sauce

There are five undisputed dessert flavors that reign supreme: chocolate, vanilla, lemon, mocha and, of course, caramel. This sauce makes anything taste better.

2 cups	granulated sugar	480 mL
1 tsp	fresh lemon juice	5 mL
2 tbsp	water	30 mL
2 cups	heavy cream, at room temperature	480 mL

MAKES FOUR 2 OZ (55 G) SERVINGS

In a heavy-bottomed saucepan or sugar boiler combine the sugar, lemon juice and water. Bring to a boil and continue to boil until the sugar begins to turn a light amber. At this point it darkens very fast—it should be a nice caramel color.

Slowly whisk in the cream—it will spit and spatter, so be careful. Cool to room temperature and pour over top of almost anything.

CAREN'S ADVICE

The only cream suited to making this sauce is one containing 35% or more butterfat. Anything else will break down under the heat.

Easy Chocolate Sauce

Easy is the first word, chocolate is the second. That's all you need to make your dessert sauce debut perfect.

1/2 lb	quality chocolate, *SCHARFFEN BERGER* or *CALLEBAUT*	225 g
2 tbsp	liqueur of your choice, optional	30 mL
1/3 cup	half and half cream	80 mL

MAKES 1 CUP (240 ML)

Place the chocolate, liqueur if desired, and cream in a heavy-bottomed pot. With the heat on low, whisk until smooth and melted. Can be refrigerated up to 1 week and reheated as needed. Perfect over ice cream or fresh fruit.

CAREN'S ADVICE

Chocolate sauce is so easy and fast to make, it seems silly to ever consider purchasing a bottled variety. The smooth silky taste of chocolate can be accented by the addition of liqueur. Choose your liqueur to suit the dessert. If you prefer plain sauce, simply omit the liqueur.

Fresh Fruit Sauce

Any ripe fresh fruit makes for an easy fruit sauce.

2 cups	ripe fruit (mango, strawberries, kiwi, papaya, etc)	480 mL
$^1/_2$ cup	sugar	120 mL

MAKES 12 OZ (340 ML)

Place the desired fruit, peeled if necessary, in the bowl of a Cuisinart. Purée, then add the sugar. Adjust the amount of sugar up or down, depending on the sweetness of the fruit. Refrigerate until serving. Can be refrigerated for up to 1 week or frozen for 1 month.

Fresh Peach and Champagne Sauce

What a wonderful combination! Just when the peaches begin to soften and are no longer fit for fruit salad, Champagne steps in to give rebirth to summer's finest fruit.

3	large fresh peaches, peeled	3
$^1/_4$ cup	sugar (start with this amount and add more depending on the sweetness of the fruit)	60 mL
	splash of lemon juice	
$^3/_4$ cup	Champagne or sparkling wine	180 mL

MAKES 2 CUPS (480 ML)

Place the peaches, sugar and lemon juice in blender or Cuisinart. Purée, and set aside until you are ready to serve.

Add the Champagne or sparkling wine to the peach purée. Do not over stir or the bubbles will break and the flavor of the Champagne or sparkling wine will not be as pronounced.

Perfect Margaritas

Margaritas are one of those easy-sipping, thirst-quenching cocktails that, when made right, always lead to wanting more. I have been victim on occasion to heavy hands at the blender. By this I mean that as the party progresses, so does the amount of tequila in the mix. My advice is to have several batches pre-mixed so that regardless of who holds captaincy at the blender, each batch remains consistent and your guests stay reasonably sober.

1 1/2 cups	limeade concentrate	360 mL
3 cups	water	720 mL
3/4 cup	tequila	180 mL
1/4 cup	Triple Sec or other orange-flavored liqueur	60 mL
1 cup	ice	240 mL
	sea salt for rimming the glasses	

GARNISH
lemon or lime slices

SERVES 6

In a large jug, mix the limeade, water, tequila and Triple Sec or other liqueur together. Rub the rim of your glasses with a cut lemon and dip into the salt. When ready to serve, pour some of your mixture into a blender or Cuisinart with approximately 1 cup (240 mL) of ice cubes. Process until smooth and frosty. Pour into the prepared glasses and garnish with a slice of lemon or lime.

CAREN'S ADVICE
Adding 1/2 cup (120 mL) of any fresh fruit to the blender gives a terrific seasonal alternative to plain margaritas.

TEQUILA
Tequila is a product of the agave plant. The Aztec Indians originally thought it was a gift from the gods. It was only mildly alcoholic until the Spanish began to distill the liquid. It was then that the drink became more potent than the version the Aztecs enjoyed. The Spanish called it "vino de mezca" up until 1795 when the companies that produced this nectar of the gods named it after the town in which it was produced, hence "Tequila." First the town, then the drink.

Fruit Sangria

This refreshing light beverage will complement any summer barbecue or get-together. The alcohol can be substituted with an equal amount of ginger ale for a non-alcoholic version.

1	large orange, peeled	1
1	lime, sliced	1
1	lemon, sliced	1
6	large ripe strawberries, quartered	6
12	seedless green grapes, frozen	12
12	seedless red grapes, frozen	12
2 tbsp	brandy	30 mL
2 tbsp	Triple Sec	30 mL
1 (26 oz)	bottle red or white wine	1 (750 mL)
3 tbsp	sugar	45 mL
1	cinnamon stick, 3-inch (7.5-cm) piece	1
1 (26 oz)	bottle sparkling water	1 (750 mL)
	ice cubes for serving	

SERVES 4–6

Place the orange peel, lime and lemon slices and strawberries in a bowl. Set aside. Place the grapes in a sided tray and freeze. In a large jug or punch bowl, mix together the brandy, Triple Sec, wine, sugar and cinnamon stick. Stir until the sugar is dissolved. Chill until serving time.

To serve, add the reserved fruit to the wine mixture, along with the sparkling water and frozen grapes, stirring to blend. Pour into iced serving glasses and add the ice cubes as needed so as not to dilute the sangria.

Joyce Ross and me

Mulled Wine

The heady scent of this warming beverage fills a room with welcome. I love serving it over the Christmas holidays as it is a perfect open house drink.

1 cup	hot water	240 mL
1/2 cup	granulated sugar	120 mL
1	lemon, sliced	1
1	orange, sliced	1
8	whole cloves	8
8	whole allspice	8
1	cinnamon stick, 4-inch (10-cm) piece	1
4 1/4 cups	red wine	1 L
1/4 cup	brandy	60 mL

GARNISH

6–8	cinnamon sticks	6–8

SERVES 6–8

In a non-aluminum pot, combine the water, sugar, lemon, orange, cloves, allspice and cinnamon. Stir until sugar is dissolved. Pour in the red wine and brandy and heat through. Ladle into mugs and garnish with a cinnamon stick.

desserts

Coconut Domes

These lovely little cakes are perfect for ending a big meal. They are elegant in appearance and light in taste.

5	large eggs, separated	5
2 tbsp	hot tap water	30 mL
$^3/_4$ cup	sugar	180 mL
$^1/_2$ tsp	pure vanilla extract (see p. 28)	2.5 mL
$^1/_2$ cup	unbleached all-purpose flour	120 mL
$1^1/_2$ tbsp	cornstarch	22.5 mL
1 tbsp	baking powder	15 mL

TO FINISH

2 cups	whipping cream	500 mL
$^1/_4$ cup	sugar	60 mL
2 tbsp	liqueur of your choice	30 mL
2 cups	large shred or flaked coconut	480 mL

GARNISH

chocolate or fruit sauce (optional)

fresh berries if available

edible flowers (optional)

MAKES 6 DOMES

Line 18 x 13-inch (45 x 33-cm) jelly roll pan with parchment paper or a silicone baking sheet. Set aside. Preheat the oven to 350°F (175°C). Beat the egg whites in a large bowl until soft peaks form. Do not overbeat. Set aside. In a separate bowl, beat the yolks until light and lemon colored. Add the water. Slowly pour in the sugar and vanilla, beating all the while, about 5 minutes.

Sift flour, cornstarch and baking powder together and set aside. Take about $^1/_4$ of the beaten whites and fold into the yolk mixture. This will lighten the batter. Gently fold in the remaining whites. Carefully add the dry ingredients to the egg mixture, folding to incorporate. Do not be vigorous—you don't want to deflate the whites.

Pour the batter into the prepared pan and bake for 12–15 minutes or until light golden brown. Remove and cool.

TO FINISH

Beat the cream with the sugar and liqueur until stiff and set aside. Using a 3-inch (7.5-cm) round cookie cutter, carefully cut rounds from the cake. You should manage 12 circles. Spread a small amount of whipped cream on top of one of the cake circles and sandwich with another circle. Ice the entire sandwich with the whipped cream, then press the coconut onto the sides and top of the circles. Chill until serving. When ready to serve, ladle Fresh Fruit Sauce (see p. 187) or Easy Chocolate Sauce (see p. 186) on a dessert plate. Place the coconut dome on top and scatter fresh fruit berries around if available. Fresh flower petals are an option.

CAREN'S ADVICE

If you prefer chocolate cake to white, add 2 tbsp (30 mL) dark Dutch cocoa powder to the dry ingredients.

Pâté Brisée

Just another basic that makes dessert making perfect. Remember, don't overwork the dough or it becomes tough.

1¼ cups	unbleached all-purpose flour	300 mL
pinch	of salt	
½ tsp	sugar	2.5 mL
7½ tbsp	cold butter	115 mL
4 tbsp	cold water	60 mL

MAKES ONE 9-INCH (22.5-CM)
TART SHELL

Place dry ingredients into a bowl and cut in the butter until it is the size of hazelnuts. Add water and knead into a ball. Do not overwork. The pieces of butter with give flakiness to the dough.

Use this as a pie crust or tart shell in your favorite recipes.

Roll out onto a lightly floured surface. Fit into a 9-inch (22.5-cm) tart pan. Line with parchment paper and blind bake at 400°F (200°C) for 15 minutes.

Quick Short Crust Pastry

If "foolproof" is a word that works for you, this is indeed that. Follow exactly what is printed below and you will have the best no-fail pastry. It is so easy you can actually press it into your tart pan and it still comes out perfect.

1 cup	unbleached all-purpose flour	240 mL
½ cup	sweet butter, cut into pieces	120 mL
3 tbsp	icing sugar	45 mL

MAKES ONE 9-INCH (22.5-CM)
TART SHELL

Place all the ingredients in a Cuisinart, pulse the machine on and off 8 times, then let it run until the dough leaves the sides of the work bowl. Wrap dough in plastic and chill for 20 minutes. Roll or press into tart pans or pie crust.

Use with sweet fillings.

Almond Pears

If you are seeking a fabulous finale for your dinner, look no further. These totally cute pear-shaped cookies will surrender any dessert holdbacks at your table.

3 cups	finely ground almonds	720 mL
1/2 cup	icing sugar, sifted	120 mL
2	egg whites	2
1 tsp	lemon zest, grated	5 mL
28	whole cloves	28
	icing sugar for dusting	

MAKES 24–30 COOKIES

Grind the almonds in a Cuisinart then transfer to a mixing bowl. Add the icing sugar and mix together. Lightly beat the egg whites and add to the almond mixture along with the lemon zest. Dampen your hands with water and spoon a large tablespoon of dough into your hands. Shape into small pears and place onto a parchment-lined cookie sheet or silicone baking sheet. Insert a clove into the top of each pear to resemble a stem. Bake at 325°F (165°C) for 15–20 minutes. Once the pears have cooled, dust them liberally with icing sugar. Arrange in a single layer in a box or tin.

Florentines

Florentines are a long-time favorite of mine. Most recipes use an abundance of colored artificial fruits which I do not like. My version incorporates Okanagan sun-dried fruits, organic raisins and, of course, premium chocolate to make them irresistible. Do not wait for the holidays or other festive occasions to whip these up. Any Tuesday night will do!

1/4 cup	currants or sun-dried blueberries	60 mL
1/4 cup	sun-dried cranberries	60 mL
1/2 cup	sun-dried cherries, snipped into small pieces	120 mL
1/4 cup	sultanas	60 mL
3/4 cup	flaked almonds, toasted	180 mL
1/2 cup	condensed sweetened milk	120 mL
1/2 lb	premium dark chocolate, melted	225 g

MAKES 24

Preheat the oven to 350°F (175°C). Combine the fruits and nuts in a large bowl, pour in the condensed milk and stir well to combine. Drop by small teaspoons onto a cookie sheet lined with parchment or a silicone baking sheet.

Bake in the oven for about 10 minutes, or until lightly browned. Let the cookies cool on the tray. If they seem to spread out a lot during the baking process, push them back into shape while they are still warm.

Once they are cool, spread the flat side of the florentine with the melted chocolate. If you are a perfectionist, take the tines of a fork and make the traditional wave pattern in the chocolate while it is still soft. If eating and enjoying is your specialty, skip the waves and just gobble—the wave has no flavor!

Macadamia Coconut Macaroons

Soft, chewy macaroons—what's holding you back?

3	large egg whites	3
³/₄ cup	fine granulated sugar	180 mL
3 cups	unsweetened coconut, shredded	720 mL
1 cup	unsalted macadamia nuts, chopped	240 mL

MAKES ABOUT 3 DOZEN

Lightly whisk the egg whites, just enough to break them up. Gradually add the sugar, coconut and chopped nuts, mixing well to incorporate. Wet your hands and roll into balls or crescents and place on parchment-lined cookie sheets. Bake at 350°F (175°C) for about 20 minutes or until the cookies are light golden brown.

Silver-Leafed Pistachio Cookies

These little beauties will win you smiles like nothing else. The silver leaf is obtainable at art stores. Make sure the one you purchase is pure and edible.

1 cup	pistachio nuts	240 mL
²/₃ cup	icing sugar, sifted	160 mL
1 tbsp	nut liqueur, amaretto, Frangelico, etc	15 mL
1	egg white, lightly beaten	1
2–3	sheets edible silver leaf	2–3

MAKES 36 COOKIES

Place the pistachios in the bowl of a Cuisinart and pulse until finely ground. Transfer to a large bowl, add the sifted icing sugar and stir to combine. Add the liqueur and lightly beaten egg white. Mix well to combine.

Dampen your hands with water and roll the dough into balls the size of small walnuts. Place on a cookie sheet lined with silpat or a silicone baking sheet and bake at 325°F (165°C) for about 15 minutes. Remove from the pan and cool.

When the cookies are completely cooled, carefully brush on small amounts of silver leaf in uneven patches. Using a brush makes the job easier. Place on a black plate and serve with port or Sauterne.

CAREN'S ADVICE
Use a small soft clean paint brush to adhere the leaf. It will stick a bit to your fingers so use the brush, not your hands, to apply.

Anise Biscotti

In North America, biscotti is the new kid on the block, relatively speaking. As we were recreating the chocolate chip cookie into 20 different versions, the Italians were quietly dunking their personal favorite into espressos and cappuccinos. The one thing we can say about ourselves is that once we get onto a good thing we don't let go. So thank you to the Italian bakers for their twice-baked cookie, and to us for taking a good thing and really running with it.

$^1/_2$ cup	water	120 mL
1 tbsp	anise seeds	15 mL
3 cups	unbleached all-purpose flour	720 mL
pinch	of sea salt	
1$^1/_2$ cups	sugar	360 mL
2 tsp	baking powder	10 mL
1	lemon, zest of	1
2	egg yolks	2
1 tsp	pure vanilla extract (see p. 28)	5 mL
$^2/_3$ cup	unsalted butter, melted	160 mL
1 cup	whole almonds, skin on	240 mL

MAKES ABOUT 3 DOZEN

Boil the water and add the anise seeds. Boil for 5–10 minutes, then drain the water from the seeds and set them aside.

Sift together the flour, salt, sugar and baking powder. Add the anise seeds and lemon zest. Set aside.

In a mixing bowl, with the paddle attachment, lightly beat the egg yolks, vanilla and melted butter. Pour in the dry ingredients and mix just until the dough comes together.

Add the almonds and mix another minute, then turn the mixture out onto your work surface and divide the dough into 3 even pieces. Roll each piece into a log about 12 x 3 inches (30 x 7.5 cm).

Place the logs on a parchment- or silpat-lined baking sheet and bake in a preheated oven at 325°F (165°C) for about 30 minutes. Remove and let the logs cool.

Reduce the oven temperature to 300°F (150°C). Using a sharp knife, cut the logs into $^1/_2$–$^3/_4$ inch (1.25–1.8 cm) slices, preferably on a diagonal. Return the slices to the cookie sheet and bake again for about 15 minutes, or until light golden brown.

Ann Rose's Absolutely D'Licious Cookies

Ann Rose, aka the cookie queen at the Gourmet Warehouse, has shared one of her many recipes for what she loves to do best— baking cookies. This will assure accolades each and every time you decide to share.

1 cup	unsalted butter	240 mL
1/2 cup	granulated white sugar	120 mL
1/2 cup	brown sugar	120 mL
2	eggs	2
2 tsp	vanilla	10 mL
2 cups	all-purpose flour	480 mL
1 tsp	baking powder	5 mL
1 tsp	baking soda	5 ml
1/4 tsp	salt	1.2 mL
1 1/2 cups	oatmeal	360 mL
3/4 cup	Rice Krispies cereal	180 mL
1 1/4 cups	pecans or walnuts	300 mL
1 cup	coconut, shredded	240 mL
2 cups	chocolate chips	480 mL
1/4 cup	unsweetened dried cherries	60 mL
1/4 cup	dried blueberries	60 mL

MAKES 3 DOZEN

Cream together the butter and sugars, beating until light and fluffy. Add the eggs one at a time, along with the vanilla. Sift together the flour, baking powder, baking soda and salt. Add this to the bowl, mixing well to combine. Stir in the oatmeal, Rice Krispies, nuts, coconut, chocolate chips, cherries and blueberries.

Spoon equal amounts of batter onto a parchment- or silpat-lined cookie sheet. Flatten the cookies with a flour-dusted fork.

Bake at 350°F (180°C) for about 20–30 minutes, or until golden brown. Store in an airtight tin.

Me and Cindy Burridge

Baklava Fingers

Classically this Greek/Middle Eastern dessert is made rather rustically in a baking pan, layered up family style and served as such. I have chosen to dress up its presentation. But don't worry, that familiar flavor of nuts, syrup and filo is just as you remember—I've just provided a new dress.

¹/₂ lb	pkg filo pastry sheets	225 g
2 cups	pistachio nuts, toasted and chopped	480 mL
¹/₄ cup	sugar	60 mL
1 tbsp	ground cinnamon	15 mL
1 cup	unsalted butter, melted	240 mL

SYRUP

1¹/₂ cups	water	360 mL
1¹/₂ cups	sugar	360 mL
¹/₂ cup	honey	120 mL
1	lemon, sliced	1
2	whole cloves	2
1	cinnamon stick, 4-inch (10-cm) piece	1
3 tbsp	brandy (optional)	45 mL

SERVES 6–8

Open the filo, cut it in half widthwise, wrap and chill or freeze one half for another use. Cover the half you are working on with a dampened tea towel. Mix the nuts, sugar and cinnamon in a bowl. Lay one sheet of filo at a time on your work surface, covering the rest with the dampened towel. Brush the sheet with melted butter, then sprinkle about 2 tbsp (30 mL) of the nut mixture over the middle third of the pastry. Fold the bottom piece of the filo over to cover the nuts, then fold over the top third. Lay the handle of a wooden spoon across the pastry, then roll the filo around the handle. Stand the spoon on end and squeeze the pastry finger off the handle. Lay on a cookie sheet, brushing all over with the melted butter. Repeat until all the ingredients are used. Bake at 375°F (190°C) for 12–15 minutes, or until golden brown. Cool in the tray.

To make the syrup, combine the water, sugar, honey, lemon, cloves and cinnamon in a small pot and bring to a boil. Once it begins to boil, reduce to a simmer for about 15 minutes. The mixture should be syrupy. Add the brandy if you wish. Cool. Transfer the baked filo fingers to a serving dish with sides. Pour the syrup over top, turning the fingers until well soaked. Can be made up to 2 days in advance.

Me and Umberto Menghi

Lemon Pepper Shortbread

Pepper provides the twist on this shortbread. Don't fret, it really is delicious and not at all overwhelming. The gold flakes elevate this to culinary royalty.

8 oz	unsalted butter	225 g
1/2 cup	granulated sugar	120 mL
2 cups	unbleached all-purpose flour	480 mL
1/4 cup	rice flour	60 mL
3 tsp	lemon rind, finely grated	15 mL
1 tsp	pure vanilla extract (see p. 28)	5 mL
1 tsp	freshly ground Malabar or tellicherry pepper	5 mL
pinch	of sea salt	
1/2 lb	chocolate, semi-sweet or bittersweet, melted	225 g
	edible gold flakes for decoration	

MAKES 24 COOKIES

Cream the butter with a mixer, add the sugar and mix for about 2 minutes. Add the flours, lemon rind, vanilla, pepper and salt. Continue to mix on low speed for 4–5 minutes.

Remove from the bowl and roll out onto a lightly floured surface, about 1/4 inch (.5 cm) thick. Cut out using shaped cookie cutters. Place on a parchment-lined cookie sheet and chill for 1 hour. Bake at 300°F (150°C) for about 45 minutes. The cookies should remain pale in color. Cool.

Dip half of each cookie in melted chocolate, lay it on the parchment paper and sprinkle with the gold flakes. Let the chocolate harden before storing.

Banana Caramel Tart

Bananas and caramel could possibly be a perfect marriage, if ever there was one. But then again, caramel sauce makes everything right, even straight out of the pan.

PASTRY

1 cup	unbleached flour	240 mL
¹/₂ cup	cold unsalted butter, cut into pieces	120 mL
3 tbsp	icing sugar	45 mL
2 tbsp	ground hazelnuts	30 mL

FILLING

2 cups	mascarpone cheese	480 mL
¹/₄ cup	Frangelico liqueur	60 mL
¹/₄ cup	icing sugar	60 mL
¹/₄ cup	ground hazelnuts, toasted	60 mL
3	bananas, sliced thinly	3

CARAMEL SAUCE

2 cups	sugar	480 mL
1 tsp	fresh lemon juice	5 mL
2 tbsp	water	30 mL
2 cups	heavy cream, room temperature	480 mL

MAKES ONE 9-INCH (22.5-CM) OR SIX 4-INCH (10-CM) TARTS

PASTRY

Place the flour, butter, icing sugar and hazelnuts in the bowl of a Cuisinart fitted with a metal blade. Pulse the machine 8–10 times to break up the butter, then let the machine run until the dough forms a ball on the side of the bowl. Wrap in plastic wrap and chill for 15 minutes.

Roll the dough out onto a lightly floured board and, using a cookie cutter, cut to fit six 4-inch (10-cm) individuals tarts. Alternatively, make one 8- or 9-inch (20- or 22.5-cm) tart. Line the tart with parchment paper and fill with baking weights. Bake at 400°F (200°C) for 12–15 minutes. Remove weights and set aside until serving.

FILLING

Mix the mascarpone, Frangelico, icing sugar and hazelnuts together. Divide evenly into the individual shells or spread evenly into the single large serving. Place the sliced bananas on top in an overlapping decorative pattern.

CARAMEL SAUCE

In a heavy-bottomed saucepan or sugar boiler combine the sugar, lemon juice and water. Bring to a boil and continue to boil until the sugar begins to turn a light amber. At this point it darkens very fast—it should be a nice caramel color.

Slowly whisk in the cream—it will spit and spatter, so be careful. Cool to room temperature and pour over top of the bananas.

CAREN'S ADVICE

The pastry is extremely short, so if rolling it is difficult, simply press the dough into the pan. It's foolproof.

Chocolate Lemon-Lime Cups

CHOCOLATE CUPS

¹/₂ lb	90% bittersweet chocolate or premium 70% chocolate, *SCHARFFEN BERGER, CALLEBAUT,* or *VALROHNA*	225 g
1 cup	coconut, flaked	240 mL
¹/₂ cup	amaretti or ginger cookies, pounded into crumbs	120 mL

LEMON-LIME FILLING

8 tbsp	unsalted butter	120 mL
3	egg yolks	3
1 cup	granulated sugar	240 mL
pinch	of sea salt	
3 tbsp	fresh lime juice	45 mL
3 tbsp	fresh lemon juice	45 mL
3	whole eggs	3
1 tsp	fine lemon zest	5 mL
1 tsp	fine lime zest	5 mL

MERINGUE

4	egg whites	4
1 tsp	cream of tartar	5 mL
4 tbsp	fine granulated sugar	60 mL

SERVE 6–8

CHOCOLATE CUPS

Melt the chocolate in a double boiler, add the coconut and cookie crumbs. Mix until combined. Line mini muffin pans with plastic wrap, or use silicone mini muffin forms. Press the chocolate mixture into the pan, pressing on the sides forming a cup. Set aside until set or chill for 10 minutes in the refrigerator to set quicker. To remove, simply peel off the plastic wrap or bend back the silicone form.

LEMON-LIME FILLING

Place the butter, egg yolks, sugar, salt, lime and lemon juice, whole eggs and lemon and lime zest in the top of a double boiler. Whisk over simmering heat until the curd is thick enough to coat the back of a spoon. Cover and chill until ready to serve. Spoon the curd into the prepared chocolate cups.

MERINGUE

Beat the whites until foamy, then add the cream of tartar. Slowly add the sugar, beating all the time until firm peaks form. Fit a piping bag with a star tip and fill with meringue. Pipe the meringue onto the lemon-lime curd-filled chocolate cups. Using a small propane hand torch, or a preheated broiler, brown the meringue until golden brown. Serve.

Chocolate Nut Rum Gateau

I call this my almost flourless cake. It is an easy cake to make, with the chocolate glaze providing a shiny crown of glory, not to mention what it does for your taste buds!

CAKE

4	large eggs, separated	4
3/4 cup	sugar	175 mL
3 tbsp	dark rum	45 mL
2 cups	ground pecans or hazelnuts	480 mL
1 tbsp	flour	15 mL

GLAZE

1/3 cup	light cream or coffee cream	75 mL
2 tbsp	dark rum (optional)	30 mL
2 tsp	instant espresso powder	10 mL
1/2 lb	premium quality chocolate, *SCHARFFEN BERGER (70%)*	225 g
1 cup	toasted nuts, your choice (optional)	240 mL
1/2 cup	heavy whipping cream	120 mL

GARNISH

8	pecans, halved, toasted	8
8	whole coffee beans	8

SERVES 8

CAKE

Preheat your oven to 350°F (180°C). Grease and flour a 10-inch (25-cm) springform pan. Set aside.

For the cake, beat the egg whites until stiff but not dry. Set aside. Beat the egg yolks, sugar and rum until light and lemon colored, about 5 minutes. Fold the nuts and flour into the yolk mixture, then add 1/3 of the beaten whites and mix. Taking care, fold in the remaining 2/3, trying to keep the batter light.

Turn into the prepared pan and bake for 30–35 minutes, or until a toothpick inserted in the center comes out clean. Cool in the pan, then release the cake onto your serving plate.

GLAZE

For the glaze, place the light cream, rum, espresso powder and chocolate in a heavy-bottomed saucepan. Simmer on low heat until the glaze is melted and smooth. When cooled, but still liquid, pour over the cake in an even coating. If desired, chop 1 cup (240 mL) toasted nuts and press evenly into the sides of the cake.

Whip the cream, place in a piping bag fitted with a star tip and pipe 8 rosettes on the top of the cake. Garnish each rosette with a pecan half and a coffee bean.

Me and Romy Prasard (Mexico City, Chef Exchange)

Fresh Lemon Tart

Lemon is one of the four most popular flavors. Once you taste the fresh taste of lemon in this tart you will understand why.

PÂTÉ BRISÉE

1²/₃ cup	flour	400 mL
pinch	of salt	
1 tbsp	icing sugar	15 mL
6 oz	cold butter	170 mL
4¹/₂ tbsp	ice water	67.5 mL

FILLING

4	large eggs, separated	4
6 tbsp	granulated sugar	90 mL
2 oz	butter	50 g
²/₃ cup	fresh lemon juice	160 mL
pinch	of sea salt	
¹/₂ cup	berry sugar	120 mL

GARNISH

¹/₂ cup	whipped cream or Crème Fraîche (see p. 180)	120 mL
2 tbsp	icing sugar	30 mL
8	candied violets or fresh edible flowers (see p. 109)	8
	fresh raspberries (optional)	

SERVES 8-10

PÂTÉ BRISÉE

Place the flour, salt, sugar and butter in the Cuisinart and pulse about 10 times. The mixture should be mealy. With the motor running, pour in the water. When the dough forms a ball, stop the machine and remove. Roll the dough into a circle large enough to fit an 11 or 12 inch (27.5 or 30 cm) French tart pan (with removable base). Reinforce the sides of the tart by adding excess dough. Prick with a fork and freeze for about 15 minutes. Blind bake the shell at 425°F (220°C) for 15 minutes. Remove weights and bake for a further 5 minutes (see below). Remove from the oven and cool before filling.

FILLING

Beat the egg yolks and 6 tbsp (90 mL) of granulated sugar together until light and lemon colored, about 5 minutes. Pour this mixture into a saucepan (non-aluminum), add the butter and lemon juice and cook on low heat until the mixture thickens, about 5 minutes. Pour into a bowl, place a buttered round of parchment paper on top and chill completely.

Preheat the oven to 375°F (190°C). Beat the egg whites with the salt until soft peaks form. Add the berry sugar a little at a time, beating until the whites are firm and shiny. Use a small portion of the whites to lighten the yolk mixture a little. Fold in the remaining whites and pour into the baked prepared shell.

Bake for 15 minutes or until puffed and golden. Cool. Garnish with whipped cream or Crème Fraîche, a dusting of icing sugar and candied violets, or fresh raspberries if in season.

CAREN'S ADVICE

Blind baking is a term used to describe baking a tart or pie shell without filling. The primary purpose is so the pastry remains crisp and flaky. The uncooked shell is lined with parchment paper, then filled with weights, i.e. beans, rice or commercially purchased ceramic weights. When the shell is cooked, remove the weights and proceed with the recipe.

Use up any leftover filling by spooning into glass parfait dishes and chilling until set. Fresh raspberries in season are a nice addition.

Italian Lemoncello Cake

Lemoncello is a wonderful Italian liqueur basing its intense flavor on lemon. It is available in specialty stores and is well worth the hunt! If you don't have it, just use fresh lemon juice.

¹/₂ lb	unsalted butter	225 g
2 cups	granulated sugar	480 mL
4	eggs	4
1	egg yolk	1
3 cups	unbleached flour	720 mL
1 tsp	baking soda	5 mL
¹/₂ tsp	baking powder	2.5 mL
pinch	of sea salt	
1 cup	buttermilk	240 mL
1 tbsp	Lemoncello or fresh lemon juice	15 mL
	zest from 1 fresh lemon	
¹/₄ cup	poppy seeds	60 mL

GLAZE

¹/₄ cup	fresh lemon juice	60 mL
2 tbsp	Lemoncello or lemon juice	30 ml
¹/₄ cup	sugar	60 mL

SERVES 10

Preheat the oven to 350°F (175°C). In a large mixer bowl, cream the butter until soft, slowly pour in the sugar and continue to beat until fluffy. Add the eggs, including the extra yolk, one at a time, beating well after each addition.

In a separate bowl, sift together the flour, baking soda, baking powder and sea salt and set aside. Add to the butter mix, alternating with the buttermilk. Mixing well after each addition, add the Lemoncello or lemon juice, zest and poppy seeds. Mix.

Pour the batter into a greased and floured tube or bundt pan or mini cake pans and bake for about 1 hour or until a skewer inserted into the cake comes out clean. Remove the cake and cool, pour the glaze over top and serve.

GLAZE

To make the glaze, combine the lemon juice, Lemoncello or lemon juice and sugar in a small pot. Heat until the sugar dissolves, cool and spoon over the cake.

La Varenne, Burgundy, France. A fabulous girls trip based on food, wine, cooking, food, shopping and food: Pat Launer, Steffie Frieser, Marion Bucci, Donna Halkier, me, Rosemary Pulfer, Cindy Burridge, Carol and Cathy Barnett.

Holly's Coffee Cake

My friend Holly Gordon makes one of the best coffee cakes ever. The best part, of course, is the great topping. It's what makes the cake so special. So keep that in mind and don't be stingy with the topping.

(see p. 28)

TOPPING

1/2 cup	granulated sugar	60 mL
1 tsp	cinnamon	5 mL
3/4 cup	chopped nuts (walnuts, pecans etc)	175 mL

CAKE

1/2 cup	unsalted butter	60 mL
1 cup	granulated sugar	120 mL
2	large eggs, beaten	2
2 cups	sour cream	500 mL
1 1/2 cups	unbleached all-purpose flour	360 mL
1 tsp	baking soda	5 mL
1/2 tsp	baking powder	2.5 mL
pinch	of sea salt	
1 tsp	pure vanilla extract (see p. 28)	5 mL

SERVES 6–8

TOPPING

Mix the topping ingredients together in a small bowl, divide in half and set aside.

CAKE

Beat the butter until creamy, add the sugar and cream until fluffy. Beat in the eggs one at a time. Fold in the sour cream. Sift together the flour, baking soda, baking powder and salt, fold this into the batter along with the vanilla extract. Pour half the batter into a greased and floured 9-inch (23-cm) springform pan.

Sprinkle half of the topping mixture over the batter, spoon the remaining half of the batter on top and finish with the remaining topping. Bake at 350°F (125°C) for 45–50 minutes or until a toothpick inserted into the middle of the cake comes out clean.

Paula's Brownies

Chicago is where most of my favorite family live, specifically my wannabe-chef cousin, Paula. Here is her recipe for the best brownies I have ever eaten. Take heed as she says, do not over cook, they need to be fudgey, chocolately and gooey! Thanks, Paula, these really rock!

1/3 cup	unsalted butter	80 mL
2/3 cup	berry sugar	160 mL
2 tbsp	water or rum	30 mL
12 oz	quality chocolate, such as *SCHARFFEN BERGER (70%)*	300 g
1 tsp	vanilla (Tahitian or bourbon) (see p. 28)	5 mL
3/4 cup	unbleached all-purpose flour	180 mL
pinch	of sea salt	
1/4 tsp	baking soda	1.2 mL
2	eggs, lightly beaten	2
1/2 cup	chopped pecans, toasted	120 mL

SERVES 6

In a small pot, bring the butter, sugar and water or rum to a boil. Remove from the heat and add half the chocolate and the vanilla, stirring until melted. Allow to cool.

In a bowl, sift together the flour, salt and baking soda. Add the beaten eggs to the chocolate mixture and combine with the dry ingredients.

Preheat the oven 325°F (165°C). Add the remaining chocolate and nuts to the batter and pour into a 9-inch (22.5-cm) square pan and bake in the oven 20–30 minutes. *Do not over bake!* Center should be soft and fudgey.

Serve with Crème Fraîche (see p. 180).

CAREN'S ADVICE

For a fancier version, try spooning the batter into pyramid-shaped silicone baking pans. They release magically, giving you a dessert that looks like it was created by a pastry chef.

Lacor makes high quality silicone pastry molds. They can be frozen to -40°F (-40°C) or baked up to 525°F (280°C). Every home cook can now reach pastry chef status.

Madeleines

Those lovely little cookies that seem to never fill you up. I like to bake them on the new silicone baking molds. They release so easily and require zero greasing.

	butter for greasing pan	
3	large eggs	3
2/3 cup	sugar	160 mL
1 tsp	pure vanilla extract (see p. 28)	5 mL
1 tsp	lemon zest	5 mL
1 cup	unbleached all-purpose flour	240 mL
3/4 cup	unsalted butter, melted	180 mL
	icing sugar for dusting	

MAKES 30

Preheat the oven to 375°F (190°C). Butter the madeleine pan, if not using silicone, and set aside.

Place the eggs in an electric mixer and whip on high speed until thick and pale in color. Slowly add the sugar and continue to mix until the mixture is thick and ribbony. Add the vanilla and lemon zest.

Using a spatula, add half of the flour and half of the melted butter, fold in and repeat the process. Spoon the mix into the prepared molds about 2/3 full. Tap the edge of the pan to release any bubbles.

Bake for about 10 minutes or until golden brown. Remove them from the mold right away or they will stick. Place on a rack to cool.

When the madeleines are cool, dust liberally with icing sugar.

Me, Jane Butel and Doreen Corday in the back. Jane Butel is the owner of Pecos Valley Spice Co. in New Mexico and a fabulous teacher of Southwest cooking.

Chestnut Soufflé

If pumpkin pie has been done to death and the challenge of a festive dessert that rings with the season is an impossibility, try this. Do not let the word "soufflé" reduce you to visions of culinary disaster, because this is not a cooked soufflé but a chilled one. Remember, if you can read, you can certainly cook!

12	sheets gelatin or 2 pkgs Knox	12
6 tbsp	water, rum or brandy (your choice)	90 mL
3	whole eggs	3
4	egg yolks	4
1/3 cup	sugar	80 mL
1 cup	sweetened chestnut purée	240 mL
1 cup	heavy cream, whipped	240 mL
4	egg whites, beaten until light peaks form	4

GARNISH

1/3 cup	heavy cream, beaten	80 mL
8	whole chestnuts in syrup or melted chocolate	8

SERVES 6–8

Break the gelatin sheets in half, place in a saucer and pour the liquid over top. Let the gelatin soften. If you are using the packet version, do the same until the granules are dissolved.

Beat the whole eggs and the yolks together, add the sugar and continue beating until the mixture is thick and pale in color, about 10 minutes. When the gelatin is soft, beat it into the eggs along with the soaking liquid. Add the chestnut purée and mix until smooth and even.

Spoon about 1/3 of the whipped cream into the mixture. Using a spatula, gently fold it in to lighten the soufflé. Alternate with the beaten egg white, then fold the remaining cream and white into the mixture. Take care not to over fold as this will deflate the soufflé. Pour the mixture into a 6-cup (1.4-L) soufflé dish or individual soufflé dishes and chill for at least 4–6 hours.

Garnish with rosettes of whipped cream adorned by the whole chestnuts. If whole chestnuts are not available, use candied flowers or a drizzle of melted chocolate over top.

CAREN'S ADVICE

Gelatin leaves are chosen over powdered gelatin by pastry chefs worldwide. The leaves dissolve without a granular mouth feel and thus produce a smoother more evenly textured product than the powder. Six leaves are the equivalent of 1 package of powdered gelatin. They are available at most gourmet stores and European delis.

Chocolate Mousse

Simple, yet elegant and light, chocolate mousse is very often unappreciated and usually for good reason. If an inferior chocolate is used, the taste will reflect it. Never settle for chocolate under a 60% cocoa butter and your results will be applauded.

My presentation of this is a little different, insofar as I serve it in porcelain tea cups. My mother was an avid collector of these cups when she first married—I still remember teasing her about them and how corny all the patterns were. When I chanced upon serving the mousse in the tea cups, I can assure you the static was sparking. Search around Mom's and Grandma's place for your tea cups. Otherwise, good antique stores often have stacks of them.

8 oz	premium quality chocolate, such as *SCHARFFEN BERGER (70%)*	225 g
2 tbsp	unsalted butter	30 mL
1/4 cup	brandy or water	60 mL
5	extra large eggs, separated	5
1 cup	heavy cream, whipped	240 mL

GARNISH

fresh berries or whipped cream rosettes and chocolate espresso beans

SERVES 6–8

Place the chocolate, butter and brandy or water in the top of a double boiler over medium heat. Stir until smooth and melted. Remove from heat and whisk in the yolks, one at a time, whisking well after each addition.

In a medium bowl, beat the egg whites until firm peaks form and set aside. In a separate bow, whip the cream until stiff. Fold 1/4 of the beaten whites into the chocolate mixture to lighten it. Gently fold in the remaining whites and whipped cream until the mousse is uniform in color. Do not over mix.

Spoon the mousse into porcelain tea cups or small serving bowls and chill for at least 2 hours. Garnish with fresh berries, or whipped cream rosettes and chocolate espresso beans.

OPTION

For espresso mousse, add 2 tsp (10 mL) of instant espresso to the melting chocolate in the first step. Proceed as above.

Poached Figs in Red Wine Syrup

More often than not we seem to run out of time during dinner party preparations. Dessert usually bears the shame. Here is a solution to the time-versus-taste war. Both sides win!

3¹/₂ cups	dry red wine (Zinfandel, Beaujolais)	750 mL
3	star anise clusters	3
	zest of one orange, cut into broad strips	
¹/₂ cup	granulated sugar	120 mL
1	cinnamon stick	1
pinch	of chili flakes	
2 lb	dry figs such as Calimyrna or Black Mission	900 g

GARNISH

1 lb	premium ice cream	500 g
	biscotti	

SERVES 6

In a stainless steel pot, place the wine, star anise, zest, sugar, cinnamon stick and chili flakes. Bring to a simmer, stirring until the sugar is dissolved. Add the figs and poach until they become plump and tender.

Pour the mixture through a sieve, setting aside the figs and seasonings. Place the wine liquid back in the pot and continue to simmer until it becomes thick and syrupy. Divide the poached figs evenly between 6 bowls. Ladle the reduced syrup over top. Serve warm or at room temperature with ice cream and biscotti.

Our first kid's class (the new generation of cooks). Me on the left, Cindy Burridge center, and David Osachoff on the right.

Orange Crème Brûlée

Brûlée, be it orange, mocha, vanilla or maple, always tops the have-to-have of dessert menus. It is very easy to prepare at home, with the exception of a torching device. The hard sugar top seems to be everyone's favorite. Ensure you make enough for seconds!

2 cups	heavy cream	480 mL
1	large vanilla bean, split	1
5	large egg yolks	5
1/3 cup	fine granulated sugar	75 mL
2 drops	Boyajian orange or tangerine oil	2 drops

GARNISH
8 tbsp	sugar, to caramelize	120 mL

SERVES 4

Heat the cream together with the vanilla bean in a heavy-bottomed saucepan. Bring to a low simmer. Place the egg yolks in a mixing bowl. Beat until thick and lemon colored, then slowly pour in the sugar. The mixture should be thick and pale colored. Remove the vanilla bean, then slowly pour the hot cream into the egg mixture, making sure that the mixer is on low. Add the oil. Pour the entire mixture through a fine-meshed sieve.

Pour the cream mixture into ovenproof ramekins and place in a sided roasting pan. Pour hot water into the tray, ensuring that it comes about halfway up the sides of the ramekins. Bake at 325°F (165°C) for about 1 hour or until the middle jiggles just slightly but the edges are set. A knife inserted in the middle should come out clean. Remove from the water bath and chill for at least 4 hours before serving. The custard should be cold.

Sprinkle the top of each chilled custard with 2 tbsp (30 mL) of sugar. Ensure that the sugar is evenly spread. Using a hand torch, evenly caramelize the tops of the custards.

Serve when the sugar cools.

Fresh Banana Ice Cream

This is a great way to use up those black spotty bananas no one wants to eat. What a score—real ice cream in 2 minutes without an ice cream machine!

ICE CREAM

4	very ripe bananas	4
1 cup	heavy cream	240 mL
½ cup	half and half	115 mL
2–3 tbsp	liqueur, such as Frangelico	30–45 mL

SERVES 4–6

ICE CREAM

Peel the bananas and cut into 2-inch (5-cm) pieces. Arrange them on a tray in a single layer and freeze for at least 3 hours or until solid. Meanwhile, combine the heavy cream and the half and half.

When the bananas are frozen, place the pieces into a Cuisinart fitted with a metal blade. Pulse 10–12 times just to break up the bananas. The consistency should be like coarse cornmeal. With the machine running, slowly pour in the cream mixture, scraping down the sides of the bowl as needed, until the ice cream emulsifies. Add the liqueur. Serve immediately or cover and freeze for up to 4 days.

Place ice cream in dessert bowls and serve with Easy Chocolate Sauce (see p. 186).

Ice Cream Bombe

This ice cream finale can be prepared in advance, giving you the confidence of knowing that dessert is done. You can even pipe on the meringue and freeze it, leaving only the browning to do at serving time. It can't get much simpler than this.

2¹/₄ cups	good quality vanilla ice cream	.5 L
2¹/₄ cups	good quality chocolate or strawberry ice cream	.5 L
10–12	amaretti cookies, crushed	10–12
2	ripe bananas, peeled and sliced	2
1 cup	brandied cherries	240 mL
4	egg whites	4
pinch	of cream of tartar	
¹/₄ cup	granulated sugar	60 mL

SERVES 6–8

Soften the ice cream at room temperature until it is soft enough to spread. Line a 4¹/₄-cup (1-L) stainless steel or glass bowl with plastic wrap, spoon half the vanilla ice cream into the bottom, sprinkle with a handful of the crushed cookies, then a layer of sliced bananas.

Top with half the chocolate ice cream. Sprinkle with a handful of the crushed cookies then a layer of the cherries. Repeat with the remaining ice cream and layers. Fold the plastic wrap over the top of the ice cream bombe and freeze in the bowl for at least 5 hours or overnight.

When ready to serve, beat the egg whites and cream of tartar until soft peaks form. Slowly pour in the sugar, beating to combine. Place the beaten whites into a piping bag fitted with a star tip. Remove the ice cream from the freezer, invert the bowl and remove the plastic. Place the bombe on a serving plate and pipe the egg whites all over, covering the ice cream completely.

Brown the whites either under the broiler or with a hand-held butane torch. Serve immediately.

Mary Selis, me and Margarita Carrillo de Salinas

Frozen Orange Alaskas

You can have your cake and eat it too! When calorie counting and entertaining at the same time, this is the dessert to serve. Only you will know it's calorific freedom as your guests will be overwhelmed by its presentation and taste.

6	large thick-skinned navel oranges	6
2 cups	Balkan-style plain yogurt	480 mL
2 tbsp	frozen orange juice concentrate, thawed	30 mL
2 tsp	orange zest	10 mL
2 tbsp	orange liqueur (Grand Marnier or Cointreau)	30 mL
3	egg whites	3
1/2 cup	berry sugar	120 mL

SERVES 6

Cut about one third off the top of the oranges. Carefully clean the oranges. Remove the pulp and juice, scraping clean the inside shell. Set aside. Mix together the yogurt, concentrate, zest and liqueur. Pour the mixture into a shallow tray and freeze for about 2 hours. Remove from the tray; transfer to a mixing bowl and whip until fluffy. Spoon the yogurt mixture into the reserved orange shells and freeze uncovered until serving time.

Place the egg whites in a mixing bowl and beat until soft peaks form. Add the berry sugar, a tbsp (15 mL) at a time, beating after each addition. Transfer this meringue to a piping bag fitted with a star tip. Remove the oranges from the freezer and pipe the meringue over the tops of the frozen yogurt. Brown the tops of the meringue under a broiler until golden (or use a hand-held butane torch). Serve immediately.

Roland Mesnier
(White House Pastry Chef, 1985)

Peppered Mango Slices
with Ice Cream

What a wild combo! Oh, where have the days gone when desserts were really desserts and pepper went with all things savory? Welcome to the 21st century where we have confused even fusion. Don't let the pepper gross you out, it actually balances the sweetness and delivers a flavor like no other.

6 oz	sugar	150 mL
1 cup	water	240 mL
2	whole vanilla beans, split	2
1/4 cup	sweet sherry, port or Sauterne	60 mL
3	large ripe mangos	3
1/2 tsp	fresh ground 5 blended peppercorns	2.5 mL
4 1/2 cups	premium vanilla ice cream	1 L

SERVES 6

In a small pan, place the sugar, water and vanilla beans. Simmer until the sugar dissolves. Scrape the pods from the beans and simmer in the sugar-water mixture. Add 1/4 cup (60 mL) sweet sherry, port or Sauterne.

Peel the mangos and slice into 1/2-inch (1.2-cm) slices. Place in the warm syrup just to warm through. Add a few twists of pepper.

Serve over scoops of good quality vanilla ice cream.

CAREN'S ADVICE

To maximize the intensity of vanilla beans, split them down the middle to expose and release all the pods once you've used them. They can be rinsed in cool water to remove all residues. Dry the beans and place in your sugar bowl to enhance the sugar with essences of vanilla.

index